An Honest Talk with Mary Magdalene

An Honest Talk with Mary Magdalene

Freedom Through Christ Consciousness

the messenger Sara Heartsong

iUniverse, Inc.

New York   Lincoln   Shanghai

An Honest Talk with Mary Magdalene
Freedom Through Christ Consciousness

Copyright © 2007 by Sara Heartsong

iUniverse books may be ordered through booksellers or by contacting:

iUniverse
2021 Pine Lake Road, Suite 100
Lincoln, NE 68512
www.iuniverse.com
1-800-Authors (1-800-288-4677)

Because of the dynamic nature of the Internet, any Web addresses or links contained in this book may have changed since publication and may no longer be valid.

The views expressed in this work are solely those of the author and do not necessarily reflect the views of the publisher, and the publisher hereby disclaims any responsibility for them.

Cover Art and Art Images in this book,
by Visionary Silk Artist Sheranda Tay

ISBN: 978-0-595-45882-0 (pbk)
ISBN: 978-0-595-90182-1 (ebk)

Printed in the United States of America

Dear Seekers of Truth,

"I am Mary Magdalene speaking through the messenger, Sara Heartsong. There is much inner work to do to prepare for the coming Planetary Ascension. Unearthing loss memoirs or the burial place of my bones is not the focus here, however if it is the will of God, may that happen as well. I speak to you now through Sara, so please have a little faith in this *method* which is known as channeling.

This book is for all *Seekers of Truth* who are choosing to hear the call of God. Get ready for The Second Coming of Christ that is you! Also, get ready to end world hunger, world poverty and world war forever! The miracles that will be coming to this world are of utmost wonder!

The Planetary Ascension is so close. Stay centered in your heart, unswayed by the fear-based news on television and in newspapers. It is extremely important to Love God & your neighbor with all your heart and soul, in these last days. The treasure of today lies in your heart centered thoughts of love and goodwill to all! God Bless You."

With my deepest love and care,
Lady Magdalene

Sheranda Tay paints images of Angels and The Divine Feminine to promote planetary healing. Her company Angel Matrix International has future plans to implement several humanitarian projects. Visit Sheranda's website www.angel-matrix.net and enjoy viewing her art gallery of silk paintings.

Sheranda Tay is the co-author of this book. She has researched the subject of Mary Magdalene for twenty-two years and she wrote a metaphysical elective college course about Mary Magdalene.

Angel Matrix International wholeheartedly endorses the teachings and truths about Mary Magdalene that are expressed here. Several different versions of the life of Mary Magdalene and her connection to Jesus Christ are now available to the public in these highly transformational times. The Magdalene is a most important archetype in these times for a reason. It is our hope at Angel Matrix International that through reading this book you will understand who Mary Magdalene was 2000 years ago, and what role she will play in the near future.

About Sara Heartsong

Sara Heartsong is the mother, healer and messenger who channeled Mary
Magdalene for this book. She is not a writer by trade. Her anonymous profile
was by her choice. The name Sara Heartsong is a pseudonym. She holds the
credentials of an old soul, grounded in wisdom and love. Her prerequisites are
life experience which developed her deep compassion for humanity. With the
help of co-author Sheranda Tay this blessed book came into reality.

Thank You from Sara Heartsong and Sheranda Tay

Sara Heartsong would like to thank her mother, father and sister for their
love and support that helped her on her journey, which led to this book.
Sheranda would like to give special thanks to Lauren Gorgo, the healer who
helped her unfold and heal with grace. Lauren is a communications master, who works with spiritual guides and Angels, using the skills of telepathy
and highly-developed wisdom. Sara would also like to thank Jesus/Sananda,
Archangel Michael and Saint Germain for their whispers of wisdom, that she
intuitively received. This book is dedicated to Mary Magdalene, Mother Mary,
Quan Yin and Mother Gaia.

Lady Magdalene's Riddles

Riddle #1: *What famous painting represents the Ascension as portrayed by Christ?*
Answer: See Chapter 15, The Ascension Then & Now

Riddle #2: *What future event, planned by the Spiritual Hierarchy, will leave the whole world very puzzled, yet in a good way?*
Answer: I wouldn't want to spoil the end of the story of history!

ProActive Prayer by Lady Magdalene:
May we all at once
Stand up on a Chair with Sister Aimee, *the faith healer from the forties, my reincarnation!*
You are her embodiments now,
and as you stand up for Truth, Justice and Empowerment, know that Faith Healing is real!
Healing our world beings with
Total Truth Today! All lies and falseness
must leave the Planet Now!
Full Planetary Healing can happen NOW!

Dear Brothers & Sisters,

"I am Lady Magdalene
and it is exciting to tell you,
of my many incarnations, in a linear fashion.
It is important to know that before I was Mary Magdalene,
I was the High Priestess, Lady Nada of Atlantis,
and I became the Goddess Isis,
and so as Mary of Magdala,
I was well prepared to be,
the Lover of The Prince of Peace,
and Jesus Christ was and will always be,
my twin soul, my twin flame, my eternal husband
and in Glorious Passion for God and Humanity,
we will always love you unconditionally.

So to complete this introduction,
also know that I have lived many other lives,
and I was once burned at the stake as a witch,
and we all know that earth medicine healers
were persecuted through religious authority beyond reason or sanity.
So why you may ask, as I am about to tell you,
that I chose to incarnate into a Pentecostal family in Canada, in 1890 and became
the Gospel church founder,
Sister Aimee Semple McPherson?
Read on and I will tell you my story."

-Lady Magdalene

Trust that this book goes far beyond Dan Brown's 'The Da Vinci Code' to reveal even deeper layers of truth.

"Believe what I say if you wish. I am not here to win a popularity contest. In the end all will be revealed and that end is so near. Historians looking for my lost writings need look no more. What is important to know right now, is all here in this channeled book. I have always been a muse, so I hope that my gift to inspire still lives on. I hope to give all an understanding of Planetary Ascension, which is not fear-based. If you disconnect yourself from fear and stay grounded in unconditional love, all will be well for you.

My deepest thanks goes out to Sara Heartsong, the messenger who channeled this book. In brief detail, she accurately channeled my life story, and then quickly moves onto the important news and work of today. I deliberately condensed my life story as to stress the importance of moving into the NOW."-Lady Magdalene

Due to the sensitive nature of this communication the channeler/messenger uses the pen name Sara Heartsong.
'The Sharing Group' *are the individuals who created the questions for Mary Magdalene to answer in this book. To join The Sharing Group's 'Magdalene Discussions'*
please e-mail bridgeindigo@yahoo.com

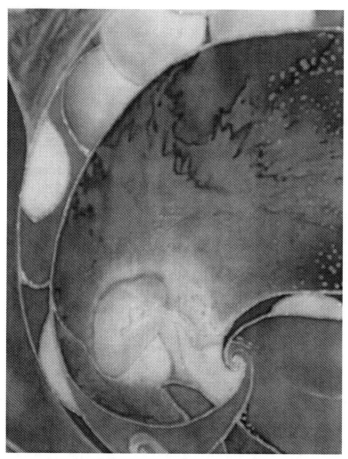

"You have become so jaded and manipulated,
once innocent, now contrived in an artificial world, Lucifer's Matrix,
wake up babes, the night has been long enough,
and the dawn waits for you in tears,
so breathe deep and release all sadness,
to birth your Light,
shower yourself in the Waters of Aquarius,
join us in the Bliss of a New World."

-Lady Magdalene

Contents

INTRODUCTION

Who was the woman, Mary Magdalene? She is known to be a common prostitute, according to a few scriptures of the Christian Bible. With the growth of Christ Consciousness many questions are being raised about Mary Magdalene and who she really was. The ultimate question, was she married to Jesus, is being explored fully in these times of expanding consciousness.

The book, The Da Vinci Code, by Dan Brown, upon its release, was on the New York Times best seller's list for 15 consecutive weeks. By the end of 2003 the best-selling novel had 4.3 million copies in print. By the summer of 2005, 36 million copies of the novel have been sold worldwide! A new breed of romantics and debunkers has emerged. The mystery surrounding Mary Magdalene and Jesus' possible marriage has the attention of the world.

A new variety of truth-seekers are turning to ancient Gnosticism which is based on Gnostic, (a Greek word), which is knowledge. In the basic tenet of Gnosticism, if we could attain enough knowledge or 'gnosis' to conquer our delusional attachment to material reality we could free our spiritual selves to completely connect with God. Gnosticism may have originally been an adaptation of Greek philosophy.

The Nag Hammadi archeological find of 1945 got the attention of Time Magazine and in their December 22, 2003 issue you can read a provocative article about the 'lost gospels'. The mystery surrounding the 46 scriptures of the 1945 Nag Hammadi find in Egypt reveals a surprisingly deeper Christ story. It is becoming undeniable that confining religion played a part in duping us, by concealing the esoteric knowledge and spiritual truths that would have freed us by now. Humanity is starting to cry out, "I need to know what was hidden from me!"

The new energy of Truth in our world of instant information has the power to transform the world. Miracles have the power to shift our mundane world. Perhaps Heaven is dancing on the tip of our tongues, but we are just now learning the language, to communicate it, so we can then express it. In the movie 'The Matrix', Morpheus tells Neo that "The Matrix is the world that has been pulled over your eyes to blind you to the truth." Movies like this clearly show that the new generation will certainly not have the wool pulled over their eyes. That is the key to our evolution and The Magdalene stands right in the center of our expanding consciousness. She stands for *your* Ascension, with as much passion as she expressed, in telling you about Jesus' Ascension! She is the symbol of the suppressed angel woman who played a primary part in the Resurrection of the Savior. The woman 'Trinity' in the movie 'The Matrix' fits the archetype as well

For 2000 years, Mary Magdalene's true purpose has been misinterpreted. The archetype of 'The Magdalene' encompasses many diverse interpretations from many different types of people. Today's modern writers are finding the subject of Mary Magdalene, a 'hot' topic. The Holy Bloodline theory of Mary Magdalene and Jesus gives biblical scholars and novelists an inviting mystery to explore. This mystery however is riddled in controversy. Perhaps the ways of The Dark, seek to mix truth with lies? Perhaps 'the truth' can only be found, with the tools of discernment in use.

Eternal Life through Ascension and how that will happen for you, should not be overlooked as the most important message that Mary Magdalene has to share with us. This transmission seeks to open the hearts and minds of millions to understanding this ancient knowledge. Mary Magdalene seeks to empower the world! She seeks to foster the goodness of each individual.

The Magdalene has feelings to infuse into you, and beyond words, she will get right under your skin to tell you that Joy and Heaven await us all, if only we could be that open to our childlike selves. She reminds us that the 'Matrix' of our modern world, will quickly fall away to reveal another world.

Lady Magdalene:

"The myths, legends and many imagined realities of my life and the time in my life that I spent with Jesus, vary like the rocks in a river. As the models of man's trials of love and Eternal life through Ascension, Jesus and I have paved the way. Eternal joy and blissful harmony can be God's most sacred gift to you and your twin soul. To reach this pinnacle of love, *'twin soul love'*, aspire to be the best you can be and in turn that self love will draw your twin soul to you."

"The Heaven that poets, mystics, and dreamer have envisioned in their minds through countless dreams is coming soon! 'Birth' can never be halted so expect my return with Jesus my True Love and all of heaven's encourage ... I LOVE YOU"

The Ascended Lady Master Mary Magdalene
the Mary of Magdala

From The Sharing Group:

Fights broke out in the streets, after the viewing of the movie *The Last Temptation of Christ* that hit the theaters in 1988. This controversial subject of Mary Magdalene and her relationship with Jesus, with all of its implications, strikes deep emotional chords in many.

A brave author from Washington named Margaret Starbird has written several book about Mary Magdalene since the early 90's. She has shaken the Catholic community with her claim that Mary Magdalene was married to Jesus. Through the fires of ridicule, the brave Margaret Starbird continues to educate the public about Mary Magdalene. She holds the belief that Mary Magdalene and Jesus were married and had children together.

To quote Margaret Starbird this is the "greatest story never told." This book seeks to touch your heart and give you the complete truth. This great story, never told, is about to be told by Mary Magdalene herself. The information in this book cannot be denied.

Mary Magdalene is the eternal *Twin Soul* of Jesus and this channeled book gives an understanding of their relationship then and now. The legend of Mary Magdalene and Jesus, touches us deeply. As major *archetypes*, Jesus and Mary Magdalene, teach us through being the *mirrors* for our growth. Our capacity to hear the *truth* is expanding as we fill our cleared Holy Grail Vessels* with *Light*.

If this controversial material is not valid in our truth, I challenge you to read it anyway. To quote a friend of mine, "The information given here just makes sense, and it rings true in my heart. The *Proof is in the Heart*. This transmission will probably be ridiculed and possibly banned by your church. However, consider what it might mean to you. Did Jesus have a wife? Why wouldn't he have?"

The Da Vinci Code, by Dan Brown has opened the minds of millions to the possibility that Jesus and Mary Magdalene were very connected, spiritually and possibly married. I am sure that this book will fulfill its controversial purpose and bring *light* and understanding to the unbelievers.

No other book, fiction movie, documentary, web-page, or religious artifacts have ever been so complete and true, in communicating the truth to the world about the relationship between Mary Magdalene and Jesus. These writings are surprising, compelling, and romantic. We hope that the warmth and love of the Female Christ, your Lady Magdalene, touches you deeply. She wishes to share with you the truth about her Twin Soul* love relationship with your Christ Jesus. In this transmission she shares her deep spiritual love for God and for all of humanity.

Imagine the next stage of our evolution, 'Heaven on Earth', to be the reward of our making. Through raising awareness, many people today are changing the world for the good of all. Image a future *Heaven* here on *Earth* filled with so much love and compassion that no one on the entire planet ever goes hungry or has to endure unbearable sickness through diseases of the mind, body, or spirit. Image that this world without greed is so possible with the growth of love that is happening right now! Image a world were sensitive people love and live in complete harmony with nature. In the future, '*The Light*' of our collective God-selves will shine bright!

Christ Consciousness represents honoring the diversity of this planet and loving every single human being, regardless of their race or religion. Christ Consciousness represents the true Mary Magdalene and the true Jesus. They see you as the new Christed beings, and it is through your actions that God's ways will manifest fully on this planet.

Look into the eyes of a child and see the divinity there, and really try to feel how much God is manifest in all of us. We are blessed to be united with our Christ, because he and she love us immensely and they love that you will finally know of their oneness.

The childlike heart in us all, has good reason to get excited and rejoice, because the one we call Jesus has a loving eternal wife, who loves us just as much as he does. Jesus and Mary Magdalene are forever in love with each other and this only enhances their incredible service to God and humanity. This is the way they would like you to picture them.

Mary Magdalene hopes no one will feel that this book is seeking to destroy his or her religion. That is not the purpose. Many of your time-honored religious beliefs may alter as a result of reading this, but this is a good thing. Remember that a bigger and more complete *truth* can enhance us and propel our spiritual evolution.

To quote Beverly Gaventa from a Time magazine article dated March 2005, Mary Magdalene is a female biblical figure "about whom we know next to nothing." Well Beverly Gaventa, Mary Magdalene is about to tell you everything about her life, her soul, and her twin soul, Jesus Christ. May you embrace this beautiful, romantic, and esoteric mystery. May the real Mary Magdalene enlighten and inspire you to go within, and find out what Ascension means for you. God blesses us all!

> With Love and Light,
> *The Sharing Group*

INTRODUCING
THE SHARING GROUP

This channeled transmission was written in a question and answer format. The Sharing Group, is the name for the group of individuals who worked as a team to come up with the questions that they felt humanity would want answers to. These individuals deliberately created very provocative and controversial questions to help bring out complete *truth* in spite of the fact that offense may be taken in the hearing of these truths. Therefore, this is not for the timid.

Not all of the individuals of The Sharing Group were available during every channeling session that made up this book. For that reason we decided to title each question with 'Sharing ?' instead of The Sharing Group.

'Sara Heartsong' (a pen-name) channeled Mary Magdalene in this document and she intends to keep her privacy intact. Mary Magdalene preferred that the actual 'channeler' be protected with from any possible ridicule or harm due to the sensitive nature of these channelings.

The channeling sessions between Mary Magdalene and The Sharing Group make up the majority of this book. The soul of Mary Magdalene (from all of her lives and experiences) speaks through Sara Heartsong. Sara's identity is protected for reasons very personal to her. Sara wants you to know that she lives a full life filled with the gentle childlike magic of nature and innocence.

Sara Heartsong hopes that the channeled messages from Mary Magdalene will inspire positive change and spiritual growth for many. She was just recently reunited with her own twin soul. The joy that lives in her heart spills over.

This channeled transmission is complete. Mary Magdalene wants you to know that the intention here is not to create a 'new age' channeling career for Sara Heartsong, or to obtain profits through 'new age' channeling seminars. Sara does not want to be in the public eye. Further channelings, are not necessary. On the other hand, there will be a motion picture created from these channelings, scheduled for release in 2008 or 2009.

The Sharing Group wants you to know that the Ascended Master Mary Magdalene wishes to be called Lady Magdalene. This is the way she wants to be thought of because she is a lady in every way. Mary Magdalene was not a prostitute. Nevertheless, she would also like you to know that she is not judging prostitutes. She stands for dignity, empowerment, honor, unconditional love and healing. She is completely non-judgmental.

Lady Magdalene:

"Judge not. It is so counterproductive to the healing process. God does not judge us. We are here to learn from many experiences. Release the pain and judgment of these past experiences. We have this beautiful gift from God to gain experience on the only planet of complete individual free will. In this free will zone there has been an extreme amount of suffering, disease and pain. HEAL and move on. Mourn no more. The best is yet to come, for all good hearts!"

Mary Magdalene sees out of many eyes here on Earth. Remember that the multidimensional soul can do and be many things all at once. Think of all time as melting together, because without time's boundaries, we can feel and be all that we are.

She is sad about all the things that crush the human spirit. She reminds us that the time is now, for big FORGIVENESS. If we view reality without judgment, and forgive each other for the eons of suffering that this planet has generated, we can get so much closer to God.

One feature of this book is that whenever a term or word used can be defined more clearly, you will see an asterisk. Look at the 'Glossary of Terms' at the back of the book to further understand the meaning of the word or term used.

Jesus and Mary Magdalene are major archetypes so a different understanding of them, from different types of people, is inevitable. We hope the whole world will accept that Mary Magdalene's life story, as told in this book, is complete and whole truth. Accept the overflowing love of Truth into your own heart. The real test of discernment comes from the heart. The proof is in the heart. Remember that open hearts and open minds will transform the world.

To preserve the integrity of the channeled words of Mary Magdalene they were not altered through an editorial process. Mary Magdalene asked that we not be concerned about the literary merits of this book. The importance of simplicity was accentuated by Mary Magdalene because the Holy Grail Legends have become so complex and bordering on an obsession. Mary Magdalene's messages are for truth seeking people of all age groups. The coming Planetary Ascension and how it relates to The Holy Grail is for all to understand.

An Honest Talk with Mary Magdalene

Freedom Through Christ Consciousness

Sara Heartsong

Mary Magdalene's World

*This painting by Sheranda Tay shows Mary Magdalene
and the dodecahedron
in the center of the painting.
The study of sacred geometry
reveals much about the Ascension process.*

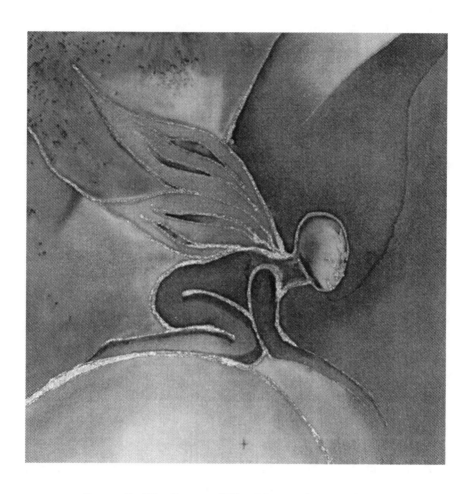

Love & Healing to The Natural Kingdoms
who have been so patient.

This book is dedicated to Mother Mary, Mary Magdalene,
Quan Yin and Mother Gaia
May we bring all the children home to God.

1

The Christ Light Birthing

Lady Magdalene:
Dear citizens of planet Earth, I am Mary Magdalene. I speak to you through this messenger to help you prepare for Christ returning very soon. Your planet is in the last days of the end times. The *Revelation* for you today is to focus on healing your heart wounds quickly, as there is not much time left to do so.

Sharing?
Dear Lady Magdalene, we are open to receive your knowledge, however we really thought the *paradigm* of the New Age movement, was that Christ would not be returning to Earth to save us?

Lady Magdalene:
Humans often think in black and white terms. Duality thinking leaves behind, the many variations in between. Do you really think that a Loving God would abandon his children? Jesus promised he would come back. Now I know him very personally, and I know that his devotion to humanity has always been flawless. His business is The Father's business, which *is* the business of the Divine Plan manifesting on earth in these times. The Father's incredible love for you is beyond your human comprehension. Have faith and be of good courage.

Sharing?
The abandonment issues we have with God, yes we need to have faith in God's Divine Plan. Are you saying that Revelations is upon us now?

Lady Magdalene:
Yes, but don't focus on this as a scary thing. You have great power to manifest a smooth transition, into the next dimension of consciousness. You will succeed in this. I am hoping to help all release their fears regarding this Great Shift that

is upon us now. It is my job to tell you that every human will rise into the next dimension, as Jesus did. I wouldn't want to let down The Father, now would I? So please let me answer your questions. I know there must be great concerns. It is also my purpose in this book to tell you about my life as Mary Magdalene.

Sharing?
Wow, where do we begin? You are expressing an urgency regarding the Ascension. Are we in great danger? Are we in such a fragile, precarious and vulnerable state, that divine intervention is now necessary, to save our beautiful planet?

Lady Magdalene:
Danger implies fear. Please do not move into fear. The intensity that you are experiencing is the magnification of The Light and The Dark and this process is natural. In other words, when a planet rises in consciousness and a dimensional shift occurs, great chaos and anxiety is usually the result, because of the added stress. It is *a birthing* and the labor pains are intense. This planetary experience is normal, natural and common in the Universes of God. You are definitely not alone. In fact right now there are millions of beings standing nearby. They are the midwives that volunteered to be here. They come from all over the galaxy.

Sharing?
The title of this chapter, "The Christ Light Birthing" gives the impression that you are speaking to Christians exclusively. Can you comment, please?

Lady Magdalene:
I am not speaking to just people that believe and follow the Christian religion in all of its forms. This book is for all people of all ages and faiths. I am speaking to women and men, I am speaking to the college educated, or the uneducated and the young ones still not even graduated from high school.

My messages are not about *Jesus Saves*, but they speak of YOU becoming your own personal savior. Your own reality is your responsibility. My job is to help all people heal any emotional wounds that are still causing, 'War in The Mind'*.

The way in which Christ is returning, has everything to do with UNITY, and the variety of different beings from all over the galaxy that are coming with him is GREAT!

So as far as the Bible myth of Christ returning on a Cloud, to gather up only Christians and then split, because everyone else is unworthy and going to hell, is just simply ridiculous! Love God with all your heart. Love yourself with all your might! Jesus is not asking anyone to follow him exclusively, as the *only way*, to God. Christ Consciousness is not about worshiping Jesus. However, it does involve the awareness of His Heavenly position as our World Teacher. And yes, He will be coming back to reside with us, because it is a job of the Spiritual Hierarchy. Politics and spirituality in the future will not be sinister or of duality consciousness.

Sharing?
We concur with that Lady Magdalene. The fact that Jesus works with many spiritual beings from all over the universe makes perfect sense to us. Are they The Great White Brotherhood and all of The Ascended Masters?

Lady Magdalene:
Yes and The Angels, The Pleadians, The Sirians, The Hathors, and the list goes on and on. There are beings that don't look like you. There is a great need to prepare. Much fear and chaos could result, if people do not understand that this huge group is working from God's Plan. They are not coming to infringe upon your free will. They would never interfere if it were not necessary.

Sharing?
What is going on? Is a nuclear war about to transpire?

Lady Magdalene:
No, that will not be allowed to happen, however the birth into the next dimension of consciousness cannot be halted. Believe me, you wouldn't want it to be halted, if you could feel the ecstasy, of the gifts God has for you. So you will go through this. There is no way out. It will happen to every living thing on the planet. Rejoice! The Kingdom of God is upon you!

I hope I can get this across to you. I am a much better at being a preschool teacher. Five year olds understand me perfectly. I am childlike. I am meek in the sense that there is no pretense with me. What you see is what you get. This is an Honest Talk with The Real Mary Magdalene. This is no joke. I am here now, through this transmission, expressing my deep passion, over the second coming of Christ in every human; *this is Planetary Ascension!*

Sharing?
What do you mean by a nuclear war would not be *allowed* to happen?

Lady Magdalene:
That is an excellent question that has an important answer. The fact is that some *Divine Intervention*, in that regard, has already transpired. It is important to understand the paradox of *Planetary Noninterference* and *Divine Intervention*. People do not see Angels and Ascended Masters. However, this is not because they can't make themselves visible to you. They can, but it is against the universal law of noninterference.

The whole point is for humans to evolve and grow through their own process within. This also applies to the Ascension process. The Ascension process is like opening to all that you are. You are like the rosebud aspiring to bloom. However, this bloom cannot be pulled open by some outside force. Only you can coerce the rose bud of your heart to bloom.

The Spiritual Hierarchy* is allowed, in these end times, to stop nuclear bombs from exploding. Other acts of *Divine Intervention* may transpire in these end times, however, only if absolutely necessary.

Sharing?
Some people believe that spaceships will land soon, even this year. This information comes from different messengers who channel Ascended Races and Ascended Masters.

Lady Magdalene:
I will quote the Hathors*, (an ascended race of beings) "We are not saviors; we're not messianic. We want to clearly step out of that projection so that the reader understands that we are simply elder brothers and sisters offering our understanding and what we have learned. You may take it or leave it but we offer it freely. In our understanding, the belief that different alien intelligences are going to save you, is just a projection of human unconsciousness. The hope that someone or something will save you, that you will not have to make any changes in yourself, that you will not have to be responsible, is unrealistic.
The belief that you can stay in patterns of lethargy and unconsciousness, then take something or have something given to you that will transform you without any effort on your part, is sheer folly. It won't happen. Now, there may be alien intelligences that land, for they certainly exist, but those humans who count on

others to bring in their ascension and elevation without any work on their part, are going to be very disappointed."

So the point I would like to drive home here is this, expect that you will ultimately save yourself, by doing your inner work to heal. Now this can be an exciting healing process; it doesn't have to be painful, or a drag, or hard.

I would also like to point out that there were (PAST TENSE) plans from the Ascended Masters for a planetary evacuation over a decade ago. Plans have shifted many times. This is a good thing. A planetary evacuation or severe earth changes are not going to happen! The Christians studying The Book of Revelations and the New Age people that cling to these old plans are simply projecting their own fears onto others and themselves. Perhaps their darkness within is what they *should* be afraid of? Doomsday thinking is dangerous and non-productive.

Sharing?
Wow, thank you clearing that up for us. We have really questioned those sources of information. We are glad to hear that California is not going to crack and fall into the ocean!

Lady Magdalene:
Some earthquakes may occur, especially in California. Pray for California! Never underestimate the power of prayer! Know that the worst that will occur, through Earth's birthing process, will be recoverable, and warnings will be announced by The Ascended Masters through your media.

Know that the best way to prepare is through your inner work to heal. Expand your belief that the world's problems are conquerable and through The Grace of God you will be receiving much help from The Celestials and the Ascended Masters to heal this world!

Sharing?
So if we use Jesus Christ, and other Ascended Masters and these Ascended Races as our role models for the Ascension, then we will be on the right track?

Lady Magdalene:
Yes, exactly. Christ is returning, will you be ready? This *being ready*, does not mean watching for Jesus to show up on a cloud or in a spaceship or by painfully

studying The Book of Revelations*. However, some day in the future, after you have successfully ascended into the higher dimension, through your own inner work, you may get the opportunity to meet Jesus, or visit The Mother Ship. The ride will get wonderful, once you have ascended, believe me!

Sharing?
Will the Planetary Ascension occur at 2012, as predicted by the Mayan Calender?

Lady Magdalene:
The time frame is not cast in stone. It could be anytime between now and Mother Earth's due date 2012. When a pregnant woman is give a due date, the baby is not always born on the due date. Just pray that all of humanity will be preparing, through healing within, each and every day. Remember that life is a journey not a destination. You will continue to evolve indefinitely. Many potential scenarios could manifest for you. Create it, and then it will be. This is universal law. Also know that your path is as unique as you are.

Rest in knowing that Christ and The Ascending Masters are working from God's Plan. The *divine plan* is nothing less than brilliant and beautiful beyond your wildest dreams! As this plan unfolds you will learn about the brilliance of a plan that excludes no one and empowers all!

Sharing?
Well, we must say that we are feeling a bit blown away by all that you have said.

Lady Magdalene:
Be light about it, please. I do not want to scare anyone. Please do not move into fear. Release the fear you hold inside.

The law of non-interference has not been broken because through the prayer's of millions, humanity has given Spirit permission to interfere. Do you see? So what is happening on the planet is a co-creative process and more people every day are awakening to their roles as co-creator's with God and with the destiny of their own planet. How many more times will prophecy shift? That is up to you.

☖ ☖   ✡   **2**   ✡   ☖ ☖

The Marriage of Jesus Christ & Mary Magdalene

Sharing?
The novel called *The Da Vinci Code,* by Dan Brown has the whole world wondering if you married Jesus and had his children. Is this true?

Lady Magdalene:
The main thing to understand about Jesus and I is that our individual devotion to God and God's mission always took precedence over our personal life. Christ and I knew before we were born that personal sacrifices would probably arise. That is what made us co-redeemers and sacrifice was part of the job. The relationship we shared from day one was all about the mission's purpose. However after the Crucifixion/Resurrection, and through the grace of a specially requested dispensation, Jesus was granted permission to married me. We moved to Kashmir, India and lived in secrecy for our children's protection.

Sharing?
What do you mean by a *specially requested dispensation*?

Lady Magdalene:
An exemption from the rule, in other words, it was not originally planned that Jesus would remain on the planet after the Resurrection.

Sharing?
In the movie called '*The Last Temptation of Christ*' it is implied that Jesus' choice to marry you would be considered a temptation from Satan, and so he chooses *not* to marry you? Why this myth?

Lady Magdalene:
This myth from The Lucifer Mind* has been very effective in keeping the masses in control, through the programmed belief in never-ending sacrifice as the path to God. Balance as a path to God would include lots of joy as well. Balance as a path to God works best; the Buddha taught us that.

The movie you speak of plays on a myth. Exactly the opposite was true. The *specially requested dispensation*, that The Father granted Jesus, had to do with Jesus releasing the imposed sacrifice theme of the Age of Pisces. After the Resurrection, Jesus was freed from sacrifice, and the next step for him was to honor himself and myself, for a job well done. So instead of Ascending to Heaven, he chose to marry me. I was forever changed by this act of mercy and grace. So with the blessing of The Father Jesus and I got married in Kashmir India.

During Christ's ministry years in the Holy Land I was his friend, his lover and confidante. And yes, this was also blessed by The Father. We were given an extremely difficult mission to accomplish.

Also know that the plan revision of Jesus staying on the planet to marry me and live a long life, had a dual purpose. The Father knew that a very human Messiah would carry much more compassion into the future. He became well grounded in the human experience by living a long 'human life' on the Blessed Mother Earth.

Sharing?
Did you and Jesus have children together?

Lady Magdalene:
Yes. I did give birth to his children! Our marriage and the children have been a closely guarded secret for 2000 years. Only recently has the truth been revealed. Even most of the individuals that were of the core group of Christ's mission did not know about our marriage and children. The strict secrecy was for the future children's protection.

Sharing?
Obviously, you *all* would have been killed, without this level of secrecy.

Lady Magdalene:
Yes this is true, the Holy Roman Empire knew that the prophesied Messiah was Jesus Christ and they tried to find and kill the baby Jesus. Had it not been for the strict secrecy of our whereabouts after the Crucifixion/Resurrection, they would have succeeded in exterminating our entire family.

Sharing?
Now that we hear the truth from you, yes, we are starting to understand. You must also understand that we have heard many different versions of your life.

Lady Magdalene:
Yes, this is true. It is a joy to have this opportunity to tell you the truth, right here and now. The truth has been shrouded in myths. The time is ripe for total truth.

Sharing?
Will you clarify with us what major myths about your life are currently causing confusion and separation from the truth?

Lady Magdalene:
Thank you, I thought you would never ask. *(Mona Lisa smiling)*. There are many myths. I intend to expel these myths once and for all. Where do we begin? How about I just answer your questions as they come to you?

Sharing?
Ok, that will work well. *Myth of The Bloodline of Christ through your child Sa Ra:*
You traveled by boat to the South of France with Joseph of Arimathea, after the Crucifixion/Resurrection. You had Jesus' child Sa Ra or Sar'h, in France.

Lady Magdalene:
That is partially true, however, further discussion will come in another chapter. Joseph of Arimathea protected Jesus and I and our future offspring from retaliations from ones who sought to exterminate us. The Dark fiercely sought out to sabotage our success. The darkness of that time was severe and the Christ Mission could not fail.

Sharing:
Were you engaged to Jesus before The Crucifixion/Resurrection? When did Jesus make the commitment to marry you and have his children?

Lady Magdalene:
He asked for my hand in marriage after the Crucifixion/Resurrection. However, we were lovers, best friends and teachers for each other from the moment we met. We could understand each other and we learned from each other as spiritual equals do. He respected me as an individual with an ability to connect with God and minister the people in the ways of his humble teachings.

I was always highly honored in his presence, whether alone with him or in councils with him and his male apostles. As some of the apostles growled inside, unable to appreciate 'The Light' of the obvious 'Divine Love' that flowed between us. They growled because I was a woman, closer to him than themselves. They did not understand our bond. They did not choose to separate themselves from *the way* their egos wanted things to be.

After much debate over who would be the leader to continue on with His Mission, after the Resurrection, He chose no one. I was the one he preferred to appoint, however, this was obviously unwise. To put it bluntly the male apostles were not going to accept the authority of a woman. Also, had I been chosen to minister the people in a murderous patriarchal society, Christ's enemies surely would have found me and killed me. So as clearly stated in *The Book of Mary** no one was appointed to be the leader, including Peter.

Sharing?
Where can we find The Book of Mary*?

Lady Magdalene:
We will reprint it in this book for your education. We will get to that later, in another section of this book.

Sharing?
Ok.
So you never had a formal, public, or traditional Jewish wedding in the Holy Land?

Lady Magdalene:
Do you wave a flag in front of your enemies, so they can find you and kill you? No, we did not marry publicly. We were always protected from harm by the loving service of kind souls like Joseph of Arimathea. His creation of a myth

regarding our whereabouts was cleverly created out of much grace bestowed upon us. The Christ Mission Council agreed to something a bit unusual.

Sharing?
How many children did you have?

Lady Magdalene:
Seven beautiful children; they were seven beautiful gifts from God! We raised them in Kashmir India, under strict secrecy, from the outside world. We lived many beautiful years together. It was blissfully normal and natural. With deep gratitude, I lived each day aspiring to be the best mother and wife that I could be.

I was consecrated by God to help my twin soul* accomplish his mission. I was the invisible woman, working with Jesus to bring you an understanding of God, to bridge the gap between you and your Creator. It was with great grace, that our Heavenly Father blessed me with a family life with my beloved twin-soul. It was the healing balm that saved my soul. You see, after the Crucifixion/Resurrection I was in a state of deep trauma. I am excited to tell you about my life as Mary Magdalene. I am very happy to share with you.

Sharing?
We thank you for sharing. Can you comment on whether the Crucifixion/Resurrection was predestined?

Lady Magdalene:
That is a good question. Jesus of Nazareth was rejected by his own people. This was by their choice, and that was not predestined. It was our highest hope that they would have accepted the humble teachings of Christ, to attain full Christ Consciousness. So you might say that through their choice, the *need* for the Crucifixion/Resurrection Drama, arose.

This act of Redemption was in need of faithful messengers to go out and spread Jesus' teachings. Jesus told us what to do, "Go then and preach the gospel of the Kingdom. Do not lay down any rules beyond what I appointed you, and do not give a law like the lawgiver lest you be constrained by it." Unfortunately, the later part of this statement was ignored.

So to clarify the purpose of *Plan A*, it was for the Jewish people to embrace their true Messiah and shift into full Christ Consciousness. This did not work. Christ was a rebel that they chose to crucify. Had they accepted him fully, the transformation of the entire world could have occurred then. *Plan B* was fully in place, before our births, because frankly, *Plan A* was considered very idealistic. The probability that Plan B would need to be implemented was very high. *Plan B* was the crucifixion/resurrection. *Plan B* was a success. What was not planned originally was that Jesus would remain on the planet after the resurrection. This choice that he made, on my behave, was granted to us by The Father. He wanted to honor me and marry me. He wanted a normal, human life. We were granted this. We traveled to Kashmir India and lived in secrecy. We had seven children. Eventually He traveled to Ancient America to spread his teachings there, and after several years he returned to me in Kashmir.

Spreading the Christ Energy or Christ Consciousness around the entire planet was necessary. The Apostle's had to go out into the world, spread the good news of Jesus' teachings, and risk their lives as well. The whole mission meant sacrifices for many.

Sharing?
You have just expressed a Mormon belief. Is it true that Jesus ended up in Ancient America?

Lady Magdalene:
Yes, this is true. And as this story unfolds, you will understand more. For now I want you to know that the *truth*, is made up of certain bits and pieces of the beliefs of different groups.

Sharing?
Can you explain this further?

Lady Magdalene:
Yes, I can break it down further. These beliefs are true:

The Old Testament: The prophecy of the coming messiah of the Jewish People, (Jesus of Nazareth).

The Book of Mormon: The belief that Jesus continued his ministry after the Resurrection, in India and then in Ancient America, up into his senior years.

Buddhism: The belief that through many incarnations humans have the task of developing and maturing their spirit, (evolving spiritually).

The Pagans & Celtic Christians: The belief that Jesus blended the ways of The Mother Goddess with the ways of The Father.

Gnosticism: The belief that ancient knowledge was taught to Jesus by The Essences and by John the Baptist.

The historical Biblical scholars who focus on the Human Jesus: The belief that Jesus was a human man, who had a human development, and a human desire to marry and have children. The divinity of humanness is beyond our current comprehension.

All Christian Faith Believers or Prayer Believers: The belief that *Faith* is the key to our divinity and salvation. Yes, it is true, knowledge, (Gnosis), is empty of The Holy Spirit without faith, (which is childlike surrender to love, trust and spiritual guidance). That is what *Sophia's Faith Wisdom* is all about. In addition, the belief that God gifts us with endless miracles, once we surrender to love and trust. The messages are simple. The healings that happen are real.

Metaphysical Information: As a precursor to understanding parts of this book I would recommend that you would read The Ancient Secret of The Flower of Life, volumes 1 and 2, by Drunvalo Melchizedek. These books are very educational regarding Leonardo Da Vinci's studies in sacred geometry.

Sharing?
Thank you, that helps us a lot. Were you the 13th apostle, and did you teach Jesus?

Lady Magdalene:
Yes, I was the 13th apostle, and yes I did attend the Last Supper. Da Vinci says you finally noticed. (Mona Lisa smiling). I did teach Jesus and he did teach me, it was an exchange of equals. Although at the time I really didn't fully embrace that I was his equal. The patriarchal age I was born into overlaid its dogma over my energy field, which later caused a problem of vulnerability for me.

I was an envied woman because of my closeness with Jesus. If they could have understood our bond through God's Design then perhaps their envy would have transformed into understanding. That is the goal now. Today is a good day to nurture this new understanding. History has not been kind to women. However, forgiveness is a two-way street. Today it is of utmost importance to forgive and release all past acts of murder, rape, violence in all its forms and hatred from your energy field. If you are a woman who still cannot forgive men, know that what you are holding onto will continue to affect you and prevent you from moving into the higher dimensional energies of Divine Love, Joy and Abundance.

Sharing?
You mentioned Leonardo Da Vinci. This brings to mind 'The Last Supper' painting by Da Vinci. So you attended the 'Last Supper'?

Lady Magdalene:
Yes, I did! My energy was really nervous that evening. I remember my *White Dragon Brother** guarding the door. As he let me in, he smiled and touched my back, which was sweaty from nervous anticipation. He knew how I felt, entering the room full of anxious male apostles.

Sharing?
Your White Dragon Brother?

Lady Magdalene:
Yes, and do you know why the Goddess Quan Yin is sometimes depicted with a White (white as in of The Light, not the color) Dragon? This is because she was another White Dove archetype like myself. For your understanding, we must next talk about my childhood.

3

Mary Magdalene's Childhood & The White Dragon

Sharing?
Where were you born?

Lady Magdalene:
Magdala, Israel (Palestine). My father was a fisherman. I did not come from a wealthy family.

Sharing?
When did you first meet Jesus?

Lady Magdalene:
When I was four years old. I was with my mother at the time. Mother Mary approached my mother and she was holding the baby Jesus. Mother Mary asked me if I would like to hold her baby. I was only four and it was an incredible feeling of the fullness of God, that I felt while holding him. In essence, I was holding myself. In my childhood innocence, the moment was pure divine joy. I felt intensely powerful and joyful in those moments. I was transformed from that experience and I will never forget that day.

Sharing?
That is truly beautiful. Were you really a prostitute? If not, why did they say you were, in Bible scripture?

Lady Magdalene:
No, I was not a prostitute. Although I was a victim of a crime that took place that involved prostitution.

Sharing?
Please explain further.

Lady Magdalene:
As I came into my womanhood, I was planning on running away from home, because my father was planning to marry me off into a wealthy family, for the benefit of himself. I objected and my father became angry. You could say that I was profoundly hurt, because I loved my father dearly. When our paradigms clashed the end of our time together was near.

I was a powerful-spirited female, and the traditional side of my father did not accept my headstrong ways. I was not going to let my father control my adult life. I was a passionate young woman and following my heart and soul meant running away. Unfortunately, I was too slow in implementing my plans. (long pause)

Sharing?
What happened Lady Magdalene?

Lady Magdalene:
You might say that the hungry lion of darkness was awaiting its feast. I was forced by my father to submit to his will. I was swept away in the middle of the night, to travel with the caravan, off to my arranged marriage. I was tense with fear as I envision escaping, somehow. Then again, my plans of running away were squelched. (long pause)

The caravan was seized by attackers, and I was raped and kidnaped, then held in captivity by the forces of darkness. A 'pimp' as it is called now, had his plans for me. He forced me to have sex with his 'clientele'. The sickness of *the darkside* at it's finest, you might say. (long pause)

Sharing?
As we learn of this, tears flow from our eyes. We are truly sorry. What happened next?

Lady Magdalene:
Now I must introduce you to my White Dragon Brother*. The man was my rescuer, my friend, my gift from God, and a member of my 'Soul Family.' This man, a Roman Centurion, heard me screaming as 'the pimp' caught me attempting

to escape. In order to defend my life, the Roman attacked the '*pimp*'. You must understand that involving violence in implementing justice was the natural way of my 'White Dragon Brother', for he was a spiritual warrior to the core.

Sharing?
My dear God. So what happened next?

Lady Magdalene:
At first, I did not know of this man's intentions, and I was shaking in fear that I was about to be raped again. However, after he was kind and offered to let me go; I came to learn that he did not intend to harm me. The Roman Centurion and I became companions and we traveled together to Gaul (Celtia). I came to learn that our meeting was consecrated by God.

So now that you know the truth, how do you feel about it?

Sharing?
Through our empathy, we feel like we were just punched in the stomach. We know all too well of the type of hurt you endured and if God was going to 'save you' why didn't it happen before the caravan was attacked. Why didn't the Roman Centurion arrive on the scene, before you were raped?

Lady Magdalene:
I believe you have an expression in your slang, 'foooo happens'? (laughing through tears)

Sharing?
Yes, but things like that just should not happen to beings of your great significance! It's just not fair!

Lady Magdalene:
Yes, this is true, life does not appear to be fair, and no matter how important your role may be, foooo still happens! True grit, is then the result. You might say that I was screwed and tattooed in that life. This is true and yet my moments with Jesus, my twin soul, made it all worth going through. My memories of our pure moments of spiritual merging and joyful bliss! The thought of his kiss, the innocence of his eyes smiling back at me, that is what fills me now and forever! Know that releasing painful memories is possible. I was raped repeatedly, but

my 'White Dragon Brother', did find me. He did help me recover from what happened to me.

Sharing?
God blesses you Lady Magdalene. We love you.

Lady Magdalene:
I love you all. Namaste, dear ones.

Power Retrieval Prayer

The White Dragon in my heart,
the protector, my yang essence of defense,
against viscous attackers of mind, body and spirit,
I am defending my boundaries, with a sword in hand
like a mother protects her precious innocent babes,
that still shimmer in the creative play of childhood.
My child, my self, I protect you.
Rapists of yesterday, your days are forever gone,
as I place you into oblivion....
The White Dove once frozen it terror, submitted to the enemy,
but now the ravenous animal nature, the hungry, control monsters of every color,
they come out of my closet today,
because I no longer need them,
and I chose power over defeat ...
defending my boundaries, with a sword in hand
like a mother protects her precious innocent babes,
that still shimmer in the creative play of childhood.
My child, my self, I protect you.

Lady Magdalene:
So now that you know that I was forced to be a prostitute, and it was not by my will, or free choice, you should also know that I was not demonic. Jesus never cast out demons from me. That was made up by the Church.

The 'The Reformed Prostitute' was the easiest way for the Church to explain why I was such an important figure in Jesus' life. The role the Church assigned me, as the 'repentant prostitute' filled their need for a powerful archetype to hold onto their congregation. You see Catholics and suffering go hand in hand and The Magdalene touches us through her suffering. In addition, the worship of the Mother Goddess truly does live on with Mother Mary and myself. Mother Mary and I bridged the gap for the Catholic Church. The blending of Pagan and Christian beliefs helped the people of those times accept Christianity. The Catholic Church knew how to appease you.

Currently in this year of 2007, all of the old patriarchal agendas are being questioned. When people yearn for truth, it does unearth, like treasures from a treasure chest long forgotten. The treasures of truth will set you free.

Sharing?
Why did the Roman Centurion befriend you, and why did you travel to Gaul (Celtia) with him?

Lady Magdalene:
The Roman Centurion was very brave, and he followed his heart and his soul. He was driven by his unique destiny that was linked with my destiny.

His purpose, by God's decree, was to meet me and eventually bring me together with Jesus, to launch Jesus' ministry. He was kind of like a bodyguard for Christ, a very important job, indeed!

Sharing?
The Roman Centurion that pierced the side of Jesus, while he was on the cross? Is this the same man?

Lady Magdalene:
Yes, you are smart detectives. Know that sometimes the supposed villains in the dramas of history are sometimes actually the heroes. There was a reason why he pierced the side of Jesus. You see, the Roman was a soldier who knew

the human body and the Roman knew that the site of the piercing would not crucially harm Jesus. The piercing was to convince the other Roman soldiers, that the crucified Jesus was dead. The custom of the times was to break the criminal's legs, and another Roman Soldier did break the legs of the two hung thieves.

Know that the Roman Centurion, working with the Christ Group*, were aiming to keep Jesus' body in tact and to reduce his suffering. A cloth soaked in belladonna and gall was held to Jesus' face, by The Roman Centurion, to help reduce his pain.

Therefore, the Roman Centurion, known through history to be the devil incarnate, was not that at all! He is the flip side of The Dragon that stands for Evil. He is a White Dragon, a mighty protector, spiritual warrior and servant of God.

Joseph of Arimathea was also working with The Christ Group*, and he was the property owner of the place where Jesus was laid to rest, after the crucifixion. The Roman Centurion and Joseph of Arimathea worked with the Christ Group*. The members of the Christ Group were Soul Family*. They have, like all soul families, traveled through time together, journeying inward. The Roman Centurion is my older soul brother, so to speak. Little sisters love protection, do they not?

Sharing?
They do. My little sister loves me for that. As for the Roman Centurion, my goodness, judge not!

Lady Magdalene:
Yes, the lesson of non judgment is so powerful here. I would also like you to know how much Jesus loved The Roman as a brother of our spiritual family devoted to the Will of God. He played the part of the bad guy on the surface. The White Dragon* is the eternal soul brother of Jesus.

Archangel Michael

☾☾　✡　**4**　✡　☾☾

Becoming a Priestess of The Goddess

Sharing?
Why did the Roman take you to Gaul (Celtia), after he rescued you?

Lady Magdalene:
There was a certain spiritual training I needed to receive, before the beginning of my relationship with Jesus would take place. That is why the Roman Centurion took me to Avalon, to receive a spiritual education. The *Druid* nature religion expresses and celebrates the ways of our Mother Earth. I was excited to travel with this mysterious man who saved me from '*the pimp*', and then swept me away onto a magical adventure!

I became a Temple Priestess to fulfill my purpose, which was to inspire and encourage my twin soul, Jesus, to succeed in his holy mission. The Roman, myself, the Druids, the Essenes, Joseph of Arimathea, John the Baptist, plus others, were all part of The Christ Group*. We were responsible for succeeding in this very auspicious and weighty mission to redeem humanity.

Sharing?
That's incredible. But, how did the Roman know what God wanted him to do; he was a Roman soldier? Was there a burning bush or something that like that? How did he know that God wanted him to play this part of bringing you together with the prophesied Messiah?

Lady Magdalene:
No, nothing theatrical, like a burning bush (smiles). He was able to hear the voice of God, intuitively. We all can tap into this intuitive power that is so foreign to our rational mind, which is trying to fit into tradition and structure. The Roman Centurion was a warrior for peace and right living. He was also a Druid, Zealot*, and a Roman Tribune (belonging to a sect of revolutionaries)

He and many ancient souls joined the ranks of many Lightworkers* after The Fall in Heaven, which later manifested on Earth. This created the need for courageous beings to work with God to bring the balance back. The Roman Centurion became a warrior 30,000 years ago, after the *Dark Ones* attacked and killed his wife and family. He was also embodied as the God Osiris. He should be honored for his service to The Light. He has battled The Dark for a very long time.

He was a well-traveled, wealthy, warrior-like, Druid man and an enigma. He honored The Goddess and he was involved with the Druids, the Essenes* and Joseph of Arimathea. The other Roman soldiers did not know he lived a double life. God had a double agent with the Roman. He was the *Protector of The Mother Goddess*. The symbol of the White Dragon* he was. The White Dragon Archetype protects Doves.

Blessed are the ones that follow their heart regardless of what others may think of them. And blessed are those that forgive the ones judging them, because the judging ones don't understand, their true purpose.

Sharing?
Amen. So, did the Roman leave you in Avalon?

Lady Magdalene:
Yes and I learned so much. I was trained in the ways of The Goddess. It was when I was thirty-one that The Roman returned for me. By the instructions of The Christ Group* we then traveled to the Holy Land to meet Jesus. Jesus had spent years preparing as well.

Sharing?
What was Jesus' preparation?

Lady Magdalene:
I have your answer in quotation marks. "At the age of fourteen, and within a year of his manhood, he began a long journey. He went into the area of the Himalayas and he spent a great deal of time in Egypt, viewing the pyramids, learning about the energies and knowledge of the pyramids. He also spent a long time in the lands of the Himalayas. He had also spent much time with the Essenes. He took within him the triangle of knowledge of India, Egypt and the Essenes. He had the assimilation and the truths of all three. John the Baptist also spent time with him in Egypt."* The reason for the quoted response is so that I may introduce the book called 'The Only Planet of Choice', compiled by Phyllis V. Schlemmer and Mary Bennnett*. This book gives accurate information about Jesus the Nazarene and about the universe.

Sharing?
Thank you, that covers the lost years of Jesus. When did you begin dating Jesus?

Lady Magdalene:
Now is the part that Fairytales are made of. I was a beautiful young Priestess of the Goddess who was well prepared to receive her Heavenly Soulmate Lover, Jesus. They adorned me; I was the 'Queen of Light'. Do you know of the Led Zeppelin's song called 'The Battle of Evermore'?:

The Queen of Light took her bow,
and then she turned to Gold,
The Prince of Peace embraced the Queen,
to walk the night alone ...

I experienced the most magical and heavenly night of my entire existence. It was that night that Jesus and I fell in love. Our Sacred Divine Union was consecrated by God.

There was not much time for Jesus and I to be together. He was a busy future Messiah, in training. He left me in Avalon and he traveled back to the Holy Land, to continue his mission. The joy of our spiritual bond empowered us both, to stay on purpose with The Mission. It was through our sharing and bonding that we connected fully to God.

I left Avalon with the Roman Centurion, to go back to the Holy Land, when the time was right to launch Jesus' ministry in the Holy Land. As soon as we arrived to launch Jesus' ministry, it was agreed upon that my personal relationship with Jesus would be a strictly guarded secret.

The Roman Centurion and I were instructed to play certain parts in public to conceal my identity. The Romans and the Jews were led to believe that I, being the traveling companion of a Roman Centurion, must be his slave woman. Remember, in those days that meant that I would be considered a prostitute for the wealthy Roman Centurion. This disguise worked and allowed me to always be amongst the followers of Christ. The apostles were expected to keep quiet about the relationship I shared with Christ.

Sharing?
Wow, this is like getting the last missing pieces of an enormously important puzzle, regarding the most sacred couple of all history, finally put together! So getting back to the story, where did you and the Roman Centurion go to meet Jesus back in the Holy Land?

Lady Magdalene:
We traveled to the property of Jesus' parents. Jesus was repairing a barn for his father when I arrived with the Roman Centurion to meet him. It was love at first sight, all over again (blushing). We spent time being in love, again.

We made love, yes, it is true! Oh my, such controversy over our humanness! However, the ways of The Goddess do not neglect the need for family planning. I was trained by Goddess conscious women who practiced natural birth control. At that time we were not planning to have a child or to get married. I used the form of birth control that today is called the rhythm method. I was trained to be in touch with my body. The effectiveness of the rhythm method depends upon clear body/mind communication, or body awareness. With full consciousness, birth is controlled by your intent. Do you see?

Sharing?
Yes, what we are understanding here is that The Mission and his ministry were paramount. You and Jesus stayed 'on purpose', and there were no marriage plans made at that time. You both were responsible in regards to family planning.

Lady Magdalene:
Exactly. And we did not need to be married at that time. We needed to stay 'on purpose'. However, to be honest with you, this was harder for me than it was for him. He was very on purpose! He was fully absorbed in serving The Father. Can I ask you a question?

Sharing?
Yes, of course.

Lady Magdalene:
Would you like to hear my short poem?

Sharing?
YES!

Lady Magdalene:
When time melts away,
and longing is fulfilled,
the liquid fire of the Twin Flame bond,
dances,
Forever still.

I Love You Rabboni, my Godman,
and while lying safe in your arms,
I truly am,
Born Again.

Sharing?
That is so beautiful! (tears) Godspeed, dear Lady Magdalene!

Lady Magdalene:
Thank you.
I am pouring out my heart to you. I love you all.

Sharing?
We love you too.

Sharing?
Were you really stoned in public? Does the Bible tell of this, correctly?

Lady Magdalene:
Yes, the Bible tells of this correctly. The Roman Centurion was very angry that the stoning incident happened. He had to watch over me while we were in public. He had walked off while I was shopping and then the angry crowd started to form. The Roman heard me cry out and then he quickly found Jesus, whom was nearby, to save me from the angry crowd. Perhaps the label of *a prostitute* would have been the understanding of the Jews on the streets that saw me as a well-kept beautiful prostitute of a Roman Centurion. The seed of the profound lesson for humanity, of not judging others, was planted through this act.

I could have died from the stoning, but as the Christian Bible story correctly says, Jesus convinced the angry crowd to stop throwing stones.

Sharing?
Was Jesus angry?

Lady Magdalene:
He felt deep saddest and anger mixed together. He cried for days. His sadness led to the birth of a storm in his heart, which then led to the bible-documented event of Jesus and his followers turning over the tables of the moneychangers in the Temple. That burst of anger and the passion expressed (exemplified by Jesus) confirms that sometimes it is appropriate to turn tables. The energy of anger that has to burn hot to bring awareness, and expand consciousness, is sometimes essential.

Sharing?
Greed, judgment and disregard for the sacred are big issues for humans. I am embarrassed for all of humanity.

Lady Magdalene:
Yes, indeed. However, you don't have to own what is not yours. You're the Light that shines in the darkness, and the darkness comprehends it not.

Sharing?
It is so appalling to now know that you, our female Christ was crucified too. Does bad feelings or anger come up for you?

Lady Magdalene:
No. You see, I have finished my healing process. The painful emotional energy surrounding that event has been transmuted. I know that Master Jesus would love to help you heal your inner child, as he did help me. For healing your inner child with Master Jesus go to www.indecontent.com/lightweaver click on channelings, left-hand side of page, then 5D Heart Chakra Activation. I am very pleased with all the healing modalities that are flourishing in your times. They are very empowering.

Know that forgiveness is the biggest part of any emotional energy clearing. So pray to have the strength to forgive your enemies and understand that the ones who have hurt, were hurt once themselves. Someone must break the chain.

Sharing?
And forgiveness is the biggest key? That's the biggest part?

Lady Magdalene:
Yes, indeed. Forgiveness and compassion grow together. Be a master of compassion. It is so worth it, believe me.

Sharing?
We are not meaning to dwell on the pain of your past, but what happened to you, after being crucified with rocks?

Lady Magdalene:
I was crushed emotionally and physically bruised and battered. It brought back feelings of my father telling my mother that I was evil. I was a mirror for my father. The way he felt about himself, he reflected back onto me. Sometimes I felt his shame as my own. This shame was originally my father's guilt for feeling sexually attracted to me, as I became a young woman. I planned to run away from home to respect myself. I knew on a deep level that my father's dysfunc-

tional thoughts coupled with his patriarchal religious programming was soon to cause an explosive rift between us. I loved my father deeply.

Sharing?
So the angry mob stoning you brought up feelings; your buried feelings of shame?

Lady Magdalene:
Yes and my feelings of being judged as evil. I began to have a rebound of hurt feelings come over me.

A broken woman-child,
I have become.
My love turns tables
and the end is near,
I can feel it in my bones,
and the wine numbs my brain,
a futile attempt,
to push away my hurtful thoughts.

He is slipping away from me,
and the Dark Forces who want to split
the bond between us,
laugh at their new prize.
My Tower has fallen,
Fear paralyzes me.

Sharing?
Did Jesus really cast out seven demons from your energy field, as stated in the Scriptures?

Lady Magdalene:
Jesus cleared my chakras, which has nothing to do with being demonic. I was vulnerable to psychic attack, because the Forces of Darkness wanted Jesus' mission to fail. Jesus was not vulnerable to attack, in the way that I was, so through me, Jesus and God's mission were at times attacked. You see, The Dark had a way of trying to trick and torment me, through my relationship with Jesus. I was not as strong as some feminists might want to believe. Jesus stayed strong

and he did not stray from his mission, but he did feel my pain. I was vulnerable to psychic attack because of my innocence.

Sharing?
So you are saying that in your innocence, dark people and dark forces sought out to harm you?

Lady Magdalene:
Yes and I was inexperienced in skills of discernment. In some ways, my innocence was a blessing but in other ways, it was my human weakness. The human side of me was trapped in the hurts inflicted upon me by my own people and my father. My father threw the first stone when I was very young. I was not made of steel, but sometimes I was good at pretending I was. Nevertheless, I had to learn in that life that forgiveness fosters inner strength. I had to forgive my own people and my own father for not understanding who I was. I was an ancient divine being of incredible power. This was incomprehensible to these individuals.

It was my love for my twin soul, Jesus that compelled me to grow in strength, courage and forgiveness. His characteristics of wisdom, courage, compassion and inner strength were also in me. Through this awareness I was prompted from within to bring out the best in myself, because I wanted to be strong like him. I knew that to nurture my weaknesses would not help him. He needed me to *not* lean on him for support. He needed an equal counterpart. This prompted my spiritual growth. This is what twin souls* do for each other, by God's design.

Sharing?
How was Jesus' mission affected by it your stoning?

Lady Magdalene:
It created a turning point in the mission. He and I knew at that point that our highest aspiration, (a total transformation of the planet through the free will choice of the Jewish people to turn to Love and Light, through their Messiah), was not going to manifest. However the seeds were planted and the time for total planetary transformation was at that point foreseen to take another 2000 years to take hold. This was a sad reality for us to face. It took total surrender to deal with this on an emotional level. The crucifixion and resurrection were planned to be implemented, at this point. As you all know, this act of

'Atonement'* would have a significant impact on the consciousness of humanity for thousands of years to come.

Sharing?
You just stated that the crucifixion and resurrection were planned, so does that mean that it was not the fault of Judas, that Christ was crucified?

Lady Magdalene:
Yes, that is correct; he was the *'fall guy'*. It was in the choosing of Jesus' people that the *Act of Atonement* had to occur. I word *'fault'* is negative, judgmental and erroneous. From the perspective of God there is only choosing. Christ's *Act of Atonement* gave the command from Christ to God, to forgive them. The Jewish People were not ready at that time, to fully embrace Christ Consciousness.

Our devotion to God and humanity was put to the test. The key to our success lied in our deep love for each other. The planned Resurrection/Ascension required that we practice through a rehearsal process. It was my job to hold the highest vision (His Resurrection), through my intent and faith. I mustered much courage and held this vision with all my heart and soul. When he was on the cross, my love and his Mother's love, flowed through him and we held the intent for his Ascension. The 'practice' of this beforehand was invaluable.

Sharing?
You stated that the Book of Mormon teaches that Jesus traveled to Ancient America? What was the purpose of this, and does any proof of this exist, beyond the Book of Mormon?

Lady Magdalene:
There is Mayan art posted on your internet that shows Christ in Ancient America with the Mayan people looking at his wounds from the crucifixion.

It is true that these travels took place and Jesus lived into his senior years. It is true that he traveled to Ancient America, from our home in Kashmir, and he returned many years later. It was necessary for him to spread the 'Christ Energy', around the entire globe. The seeds of Christ Consciousness were planted around the entire globe, to absorb into every major race on the planet. This was very important.

In the best case scenario, the Jewish People (originally from Venus), would have embraced their true Messiah. Jesus stated that he was not from the planet earth. He and I are from the planet Venus. The rejection of him, by his own People created the need for his ministry to permeate the entire globe. That is why he had to travel around the globe to continue his ministry into his senior years.

Sharing?
Can you comment on sacrifice, in regards to attaining oneness with God? Does the monk or the nun, stand the best chance to attaining enlightenment?

Lady Magdalene?
That is a good question. Some believe that sacrifice, and especially celibacy, is the only path to divinity. It is only one path. All paths to God are valid. Judge not another's way, that may not be your own.

Great sacrifice is a feature of the age of Pisces. However, in the Age of Aquarius, this will not be so. These ages are overlapping now, and *the old* is on the way out. To move into the NOW people need to stop their over-worship of events like The Crucifixion. The job at hand involves taking individual responsibility for your path to the divine. Worshiping another's *act of sacrifice* does not replace ones need to do their own inner work. The kingdom of God is Within You! Focus not on the past; move into the NOW. What can you do right now to increase your own personal spiritual progress? Be the change that you would like to see it the world. Then you will truly be honoring Jesus.

Please know that tragic endless suffering was not the plan for this planet. The plan was to develop Heaven on Earth through the hearts of men and women. This has been tough. The irresistible pull of The *Ring of Power* has stunted the growth of many. The *Lambs of God* have endured long suffering beyond belief. The 'Fall' in Heaven, is the root of 'The Fall' here on Earth. As above so below.

The beauty of this precarious free-will is the element of surprise and adventure that it feeds our souls with. We love adventure but it is a double-edged sword, it is duality. The Planet Earth is NOT boring, and we love that. We are courageous, passionate, God loving, freethinkers, and we are blessed!

Even tragedy has a silver lining! The magic of tragedy is that we get a chance to develop the deepest type of compassion there is, which is experiential. Deep compassion for the suffering of anyone and everyone only comes from feeling lots of experiences, and through many lives this is what we have done. Compassion can change the entire world and it is doing just that. This is a gradual process and it is going well. The Christ Child is very alive and well! The Christ Child is you, right now! Remember that we are all Holy Blood, of the soul lineage of God. We are all God's children, and we are all equally precious, in God's eyes.

Sharing?
Can you comment on the myth of the Christ Bloodline in France?

Lady Magdalene:
Before I answer your question, I ask that you realize that the 3rd dimensional perception is limited. You must think outside 'the box' to understand what I am about to tell you. You see, I incarnated into two women, 2000 years ago in the Holy Land. I was also the woman known as Mary of Bethany. Some who research my life believe that Mary of Bethany and Mary of Magdala were the same woman. We were of the same soul, not the same woman, do you see?

Both of my Mary embodiments served a purpose. This whole book is about myself as Mary Magdalene. Now for you to understand Mary of Bethany's purpose let me say this; she was born to be a 'backup', of Magdalene, in case I (as Mary of Magdala) was killed. Thanks to my Dragon Brother, Jesus, and many Angels, I survived three close encounters with death in my life as Mary of Magdala. This altered my purpose, as Mary of Bethany. One's spiritual divine plan can have several options. As Mary of Bethany I devoted myself to communing with The Angels and assisting people as a spiritual guide and healer. So many of *the legends* are correct.

Sharing?
That is incredible! We looked up the word *myth* in the dictionary and we came across this quote by Cecil M. Bowra; it reads, *"myths bring the unknown into relation with the known."* Thank you for clarifying that for us.

Lady Magdalene:
I thank you for asking the most important questions. I would like to clarify that in both of my Mary lives, I traveled to the coast of France. As Mary of Bethany I arrived on the coast of France with my baby Sar'h in my arms.

Sharing?
Ok. We don't mean to pry, but to whom was Mary of Bethany married?

Lady Magdalene:
God, my dear ones. My conception of Sar'h (Sa Ra) through the power of The Holy Spirit was a blessed miracle. She was created through the joining of three ascending hearts that were one, in the passionate compassion of self for self. In learning of Mary of Magdala's brush with death (her stoning), I became extremely focused in healing her heart, as it was my own. I experienced the oneness of all life and all beings living in unity and love, free from The Matrix of the illusions of sin, competition, envy and sacrifice. When you give freely, sacrifice is exposed for the illusion that it is. When I, as Mary of Bethany let go of my secret desire to marry Jesus, I conceived Sar'h. Letting go can help create the most amazing miracles! This experience was birthed through my compassion for another aspect of myself that was hurting. Magdala was almost completely devoured in sadness after her stoning, as it was also when she had to come to terms with the knowledge that her Beloved Jesus would be crucified. As Mary of Bethany my compassion for her created a child in my womb. Does this sound unbelievable?

Sharing?
No. We believe that with God all things are possible!

Lady Magdalene:
That is so true! So back to the story, I arrived on the coast of Southern France as Mary of Magdala before the blessed arrival of Mary of Bethany. Further discussion of this will come later. For now just know that God works in mysterious ways, however what appears mysterious later becomes very logical, once understood. For now just understand that as Mary of Bethany I was a 'watery personality', and very connected to Heaven (and as her, I loved Jesus from afar in spiritual contemplation) and that was my divine purpose as Mary of Bethany. As Mary of Magdala I was a 'fiery personality', and very connected to Earth (and Jesus' wife and mother to his children in India) and that became part of my divine purpose as Mary of Magdala.

The term The Magdalene refers to both or either one of my embodiments in the Holy Land. The term The Magdalene also refers to all of my embodiments of all time, and furthermore it refers to anyone teaching and sharing, through my archetypical energy.

5

Healing after the Age of Patriarchy

Sharing?
What advice can you share with us regarding the Women's Movement and the present day Goddess worship? With the imbalances of centuries, where do we go from here?

Lady Magdalene:
Like always, go within! We cannot heal ourselves without outrageous forgiveness and trust. Use many methods of emotional body healing. The men and women of today have different scars from *The Battle of the Sexes*. Women must not blame men, and men should not blame women either. The Dark Forces that devised the plan to divide and conquer, want you to continue to blame the opposite sex. Then they do not have the finger pointed at them. Their strategy worked, but now we need to undo the damage. This is going to take patience and persistence.

The Goddess worship of today needs to get down to Earth. Create ways to help the sick and the poor. The political systems and certain religious beliefs have breed dysfunctional families. We need to get back to the basic core teachings of Christ. He will be coming back to assist in the restoration of his original teachings.

Tours to the South of France are not going to heal the world. That is a nice vacation, but not the greatest honor to me, do you see? There is real work to do right here in America, and abroad, to save the environment and help people in need. Focus on humanitarian projects. The children of the world need your help. They are the future. The atrocities occurring worldwide need your attention.

Sharing?
So get down to earth, because Heaven of Earth will only be build here, one step at a time.

Lady Magdalene:
Yes and the Age of Aquarius is rising. Right now the old energy of patriarchy is moving out as the new energy is moving in. The overlapping of clashing paradigms that you see today is part of this process of change. Be compassionate and understanding to all. When you step out of duality consciousness, into full Christ consciousness and love for all, then healing can happen on all levels.

The Dance of Duality

Be patient
Love thy enemies
Be compassionate
Be not fooled by the Dance of Duality
Certainly it was duality that made you
what you are today,
a soul who chose wisely
in the valley of the shadow of death,
the death that was merely a transient point
that led to the Eternal Life of Unity
Recognize the illusions of duality
as the fruitful teachers of yesterday
and now is Graduation Day
sing praise
and give a kiss to Lucifer
He played His part well.
Forgive your enemies
and release your Lucifer Mind
type thoughts.
Prepare today!
For the dawn of understanding
is beaconing the new day....

To Lucifer

Oh my.... my brother Lucifer. This *tug of war* game has gone on long enough. The *wars in the minds* of men and women everywhere on earth, continue. But they are embracing Christ Consciousness dear brother Lucifer. The Light is winning over the souls of our family, the family that you were once a part of, dear brother.

.....Lady Magdalene

With Forgiveness and Compassion,
Releasing 'The War in The Mind'
... in prayer, in meditation, focus on these words to release the negative energy of old contracts/programs that no longer serve you.
I am a powerful being,
I command that any programs, contracts or past agreements to be engrossed in thoughts and actions that do not serve my higher good and connection to God, be released, erased and obliterated, now!
All **fear, lack, worry, suffering, grief, sacrifice, sickness, unworthiness, separation, abandonment, judgment, anger, hate, conflict, karma, imprisonment, illusions and** _____ (*add your own here*)
I command to be released, erased and obliterated, now!

I have full memory, and full consciousness now!
My fullness in The Light allows no darkness to penetrate me. I am fully free. I can heal everything. I am healed! And so it is!

Sharing?
That is a powerful prayer! The singer/songwriter Lauren Hill wrote a song called the *War in the Mind*. Check it out online at LimeWire.com

6

Christ & The Nesara Project

Sharing?
On the internet we have read about Nesara, and that it was created by Christ and other Ascended Masters. What is Nesara?

Lady Magdalene:
The name NESARA, stand for National Economic Security and Reformation Act. Christ's Nesara plans began in 1967. The end days are here and soon you are going to witness some very dramatic changes, for the good of all of humanity. This help from Christ, sanctified by God is for the purpose of bringing the balance back to this planet. Christ is returning to help, but not to fix it all for you!

I have observed two distinctly different mindsets in most people today. Some believe that God has abandoned you, and no help from Heaven is going to relieve humanity. The opposite mindset wants to fantasize that their religious devotion is going to 'save them' and give them 'The Rapture', but not the other guys that don't have their same beliefs. Both of these mindsets are out of balance.

Sharing?
This Nesara Project* you speak of is tied to the Second Coming of Christ?

Lady Magdalene:
Yes. And Christ Michael is leading the whole project. God's grace is huge, right now. The Anti-Christ deeds of *The Bush Crime Family* and the Illuminati must be revealed to humanity as soon as possible! The people's choice to embrace the truth is so important right now! Many lies will be exposed in your years to

come. All of the dirty politics of the power hungry conglomerates need to be exposed now.

Sharing?
Wow, that is great! We were beginning to worry that no one could stop Mr. Bush!

Lady Magdalene:
Well there is more to it than just replacing Mr. Bush with another president. The Illuminati must be exposed for their crimes. Many have lost the faith that their prayers have been heard! They have been heard! Every one of them matters! You matter. Believe it. The human experience makes one feel so isolated from God. This illusion of separation is going to end. The madness must end!

Thousands of spaceships full of loving, caring beings from all over the galaxy are poised and ready to help. They may appear in the skies all across America possibly very soon. An educational television broadcast of Jesus Christ may happen in the near future.

Sharing?
Why do you say 'may happen'?

Lady Magdalene:
Because you must understand that The Christ Mission plans have always been flexible. The prayers of millions have continued to alter the original predictions of The Book of Revelations. This is a good thing. It is proof positive that through the faith and love of humanity we will now go through a much smoother transition into the next dimension of consciousness. It was never written in stone that every single detail of the Book of Revelations would occur. Understand that every single day on the planet now, has altering potentials playing themselves out.

Through the leadership of Christ Michael, an elaborate and long drawn out 'Chess Game with the Dark' has played itself out. That Chess Game has entertained many 'scenarios'. That is why you may read about things on the internet, about some 'end times plan', that does not manifest. The Chess Game with the Dark continues on. Many council meetings take place. Many plan revisions happen. So the best thing to do, is to not get caught up in them. Just stay focused on your own self love and pray for all of humanity to release their fears and trust in God!

It is important that people don't mistake a possible 'spaceship armada' as a hostile takeover of the planet. Many fears about aliens in spaceships shroud the human collective consciousness, because of the evil alien abductions that happened. Believe me, the *evil aliens* were expelled from the planet years ago. The loving beings here in the skies today are not evil! They may fly over in the thousands and display a fantastic light show. This possible wake up call is for humanity may transpire, if it is deemed most wise. However, things may happen in a different way. Worry not about the how, just know that you are safe with your love-based thoughts.

Know that serious instructions for the masses are coming in the next few years. Be flexible. Things could happen next week or next year. Think of these signs coming in a flexible time frame. The masses need to understand that this world is going to shift into the next dimension of consciousness; it is unstoppable! The ascension will happen. It is God's will and plan for you.

Sharing?
Will anyone be excluded from this experience?

Lady Magdalene:
No one will be excluded. It is impossible to be excluded. But if people have not prepared themselves, they won't make it in the higher dimensional Earth and they will be relocated to a world that fits their vibrational level. So the main criteria for being prepared will be one's ability to stay centered in love, and trust God's plan. Some Lightworkers who are aware of the Ascension have been preparing for years. It does not have to take years. Let go of the past, to allow Divine Love to come in. This can literally happen in moments.

The works of the anti-evolutionary forces have made quite a mess of things here on planet Earth. Jesus Christ, now 2000 years later, will witness the effects of his Good Courage and Immense Compassion, come full-circle; as the ages change over.

Sharing?
We still don't fully understand this N.E.S.A.R.A. Project? We have several friends that believe we are nuts for believing in some weird internet information, that sounds like a *rapture scenario* lie. Can you comment?

Lady Magdalene:
Have you ever known someone with a complete aversion to receiving help from others? Surrendering the ego mindset of '*The Atlas*' is hard for some people.

A Single Grain of Sand Shifts an Entire World

The Sand Man

How did a single grain of sand, shift an entire world?
How did His passion to protect the innocent,
feed the hungry, relieve the poor and heal the sick
transform into the Hope of The World?
The answer my friend,
lies in His Great Love,
a love so deep,
no darkness could swallow it completely,
and even when his Lady was unconscious,
and sleeping,
His dreams of future joy seeped out,
to save his Precious Hope.
A single grain of sand can shift an entire world!
This is exemplified in Christ,
and through His unconditional Love,
for Humanity.

By Sara Heartsong

Sharing?
Are Jesus and the Buddha united in purpose? Is Buddha coming back with Jesus Christ?

Lady Magdalene:
Yes, they are united in a purpose. There is only one single purpose, full Christ Consciousness manifesting within every single human on the planet. The Buddha will be coming back with Christ and the entire entourage of God.

Prince Siddhartha became The Buddha. His deep compassion fueled his crusade for helping the suffering masses. As Prince Siddhartha, he fully chose selflessness, over comfort, and courage over fear. He became The Master Buddha because he was fully devoted to God's mission. God loves him dearly for his service. Now you may think of yourself as just a single grain of sand with no significant power to change this world for the better. This is not true. In the *Golden Age* you will all become Masters if you choose to. It does not matter if you have sinned and it does not matter if you have not fully mastered transcendental meditation. You will learn and you will teach. Does it seem improbable to you that thousands of Masters could walk the earth in the near future?

Sharing?
Well yes, it does seem improbable.

Lady Magdalene:
Could you practice embracing your greatness for me? Do you know what happened to the Grays (aliens) that abducted (a cruel form of rape) many people?

Sharing?
No, please tell us.

Lady Magdalene:
There was a young woman who embraced her *divine power*, and she was successful in having them all expelled from the planet earth. All the Grays are gone, and they cannot get back into our sphere. So it is important for you to know that alien abductions are a thing of the past. Unfortunately, the fear that The Grays implanted into the collective consciousness of the planet still remains. This causes a problem for First Contact*. Know that the UFO's of today are all benevolent. First Contact*, the planned flyover of spaceships, has the intended

purpose of raising the awareness of God's intervention and assistance in helping every human make the transition into the next dimension.

I have deep compassion for the victims of evil deeds. I hope to expel fear and bring hope to all who will listen to me. May peace live in your hearts, dear brothers and sisters.

Jesus Sananda Esu Immanuel
-*image by Suzanne DeVeuve*

Lady Magdalene:
Why are all these names His, along with the titles, Lord, Ascended Master, Christ and Messiah?

Because He and I are very old souls and we have been very busy attending to thy Father's work for a very long time. He is known as Esu Immanuel on another planet. He is known as Lord Sananda by the Ashtar Command*.

Why do I like this image of Him?
It reminds me of the joyful years we had shared together in India and it captures his childlike mischievousness.

A cold winter morning in Kashmir?
Yes, very cold. His breath looks like smoke in this image.

What images of Christ do I like?
The ones that capture his spiritual essence.

Why do I call him The Sand Man?
Because he was always dragging sand into the house. (smiles)

🕯🕯 ✡ **8** ✡ 🕯🕯

The Legend of
The Holy Grail

Sharing?
Can you comment on the book called Holy Blood, Holy Grail?

Lady Magdalene:
This book led to Dan Brown's work, which is a good thing. His work is based on the myth of The French Bloodline of Christ, but so what. They have got most of the facts straight.

I believe that Dan Brown's intentions are pure. However some of the writers of the book Holy Blood, Holy Grail, I would question their motives. The mystery has many dark veils. Do not trust any ploy that seeks to romance you into doing a blood or DNA test, to check what bloodline you come from. Question people's motives; what are they after?

Margaret Starbird wants you to embrace the Divine Feminine and visualize balance and peace between men and women. That is true Grail Christianity and it is pure of heart. Beware of those after your pocketbook, trying to sell you on The Holy Grail, Bloodline. What other motives might they have besides profit?

The ultimate truth is this; does a certain bloodline keep you pure at heart? No. Effort and devotion to God and humanity does. It is still the quality of your deeds of love and compassion, which earn your place in Heaven! Does God not see beyond our masks of glory? Humble love is not the intent of all the seekers of the Holy Grail.

Sharing?
We have a movie showing Indiana Jones picking from a table of Holy Grail cups. He had one try to pick the right one, which belonged to Jesus Christ. He knew which one it was, the plain one. No jewels or claims to fame, can buy you a place in Heaven, because it is within you. We see this clearly.

Lady Magdalene:
Yes, and you can see how some of these Grail Seekers are just confused, because the truth has been distorted for so long. Still, many have ignored the fact that The Kingdom of God is within!

The romance of the 'Holy Grail' has left some people spellbound. Nevertheless, certain authors like Margaret Starbird write about the subject with the intent to restore the rights of women to hold spiritual positions in their churches. This is important. Women and men are equals. Why not change your time honored, yet old and outmoded thinking.

This bold and courageous author believes that Jesus and I were traditionally married. Her church community has ostracized her and judged her as blasphemous. She wishes to promote the truth in such a way as to gain the acceptance of these church type people.

Jesus never ruled from a throne on Earth. He did not drink from Golden Goblets. He did however wear out a lot of pairs of sandals, from traveling many parts of the world on foot. The humbleness of his service to humanity cannot be stressed enough! Jesus was truly unselfish, and this is a characteristic of a true Master.

Remember that the true Jesus had a message of humbleness to get across to us. 'Jeweled Golden Cups' are of no value without the richness of the heart and soul to fill them. That is why I picked Sara to channel my messages, because she is humble, simple and a faithful lover of God, and an excellent mother I might add. I chose her pen name, Sara Heartsong. Her song, you may reject if you choose. The point here is not to win a popularity contest or to distort the truth to the liking of a particular group.

Sharing?
Can you comment on King Arthur and Camelot?

Lady Magdalene?
During the time of King Arthur the hope was to fuse the Pagan and Christian beliefs into one. It was the hope of King Arthur that the true teachings of Christ would soon be understood by way of his influence. However, as history tells us, the Saxons slaughtered The Knights of the Round Table and their army and Camelot was lost. The bridge between two worlds, Avalon and third dimensional Earth, closed when Arthur lost his kingdom. The ways of The Goddess were then replaced with the suppressive ways of the Catholic Church. It was very sad indeed.

Sharing?
The saddest part is that it seems that history had repeated itself. Camelot carried the hope of Christ's true teachings taking hold. Unfortunately, The Goddess ways were forced into hibernation, squelching the hope of *the people* learning about the balance of Ying/Yang, male/female balance.

Lady Magdalene:
Yes and the timing for this and Peace on Earth was again set into the far away future. The seeds of *Love* and *Peace* were still not developed enough to sprout and grow into full maturity. Nevertheless, the legendary Celtic People kept the precious seeds of Christ's true teachings deep within their hearts.

Understand that The Nazarene, as prophesied by the Three Wise Men, came to rule his own people. The Jewish People are from Venus. Jesus' mission was targeted to his own people. He came to transform the hearts of his own people. The Jewish people rejected this fact because they were emotionally close-hearted, stubborn and stuck in their religious traditions. However, after they rejected Christ, we carried the vision in our hearts to transform the rest of the world's people. He was not bound to his own people after the Crucifixion/ Resurrection. The Celts, and the Gypsies embraced the radical Jesus willingly. They loved The Mother Goddess as well. They created a fusion of Christian and Pagan ways.

Sharing?
Well, we are very enlightened to finally hear your true story, Lady Magdalene. I know that all who worship the Goddess will be pleased to hear how Jesus' support has been there all along. The Celts are famous for being passionate about the God/Goddess Union, in thought and feeling.

Sharing?
What is the significance of The Holy Grail today?

Lady Magdalene:
As always, it is universally the quest to find God within and become a co-creator with God. It is the ultimate path to Divine Love and freedom. It is your Divine Birthright.

Sharing?
It is understood by some that *you* were the Holy Grail, in that you carried the Holy Blood of Christ in your womb, and by birthing his children, his Bloodline would live on.

Lady Magdalene:
Yes that is true as well. However, the significance of that truth does not hold a sacred personal meaning for everyone. It should not. If it does for you then you may be a descendant of Christ with a sacred agreement to help spread the truth about Christ's true teachings. If you all would realize that we are all of the soul lineage of God, you would simple say, I don't care about this whole Bloodline distraction, let's just get down to business!

I am the Co-redeemer standing beside my husband as his spiritual equal. Now this is a very taboo concept to most of the world. However, the times are changing rapidly.

Sharing
That is an understatement.

Lady Magdalene:
Yes indeed. So can you understand that Legend and Myth can be very instrumental in creating change. Whether all of the facts of a myth are true, well, sometimes it doesn't matter. If it leads to total truth and enlightenment, it is a good thing.

Know that there were two types of Holy Grail seekers. The humble seekers know that the pursuit of the Holy Grail is an endless journey inward, which leads to Divine Union with God.

Now it should be understood that the Ascended Masters that have achieved a high level of spiritually are very ancient souls. Know that God hands the Holy Grail to no one on a silver platter. Remember that the journey to Divine Union with God is just as important as the destination. Also know that I am just as ancient a soul as my Beloved, because twin souls share the same soul birth date; do you see?

Sharing?
Yes, we do, and there is no *instant coffee* path to God! We certainly can understand that as well.

Lady Magdalene:
Some people get caught up in The Dark's ploy to sell them on an '*instant gratification version of divinity*' that is not even based on spiritual principles or disciplines. This type of Holy Grail seeker thinks that all that glitters is gold.

Sharing?
And to quote Led Zeppelin, "*and she's buying the stairway to Heaven*"

Lady Magdalene:
When a song like that gives you truth bumps, you know it contains an extremely significant truth for humanity.

Know that many gurus and false Christs in these times are out to deceive you, and lead you astray. Some of these New Age movement gurus have made a tidy profit out of preying on spiritual seekers. I trust that by now you will see them for their works, as my Beloved once told you. However, deciphering fact from fiction is hard, because The Dark use so many smoke screens and mirrors to confuse you! They also mix much truth with fiction, to convince you that the whole package they are selling you on, is true. This is a common 'Christian cult'* attribute.

Just know that anything associated with The Knights Templar, you should question. Evil and Good can be all mixed together sometimes. This gives The Dark the advantage of confusion. People tend to look at surface appearance. It would be wise to take a course on critical thinking.

Know that the Holy Grail Christ Child* is the one that is alive in your heart! Hearts that link together with Christ through his purposes are the true family of Christ, and the ones whom he would befriend.

Know that Christ and I advocate the end of suffering for all. So accept the Holy Sacred Mother and The Father, into your own heart and mind. I would like to see all brothers and sisters graduate from this third dimensional, limited reality. Will you help me? Will you help spread the word about The True Christ Child that has the potential to ascend, when Mother Earth Ascends? This event is coming soon. Will you be ready?

I challenge you to fill your own Holy Grail, your Body Temple* with so much love, compassion, forgiveness and generosity, as to Light this World Up! Be the Lighthouse. Be the one carrying another across the sand, because they are too weak and they needed you. Be a part of the Christ Family today, through your deeds! We welcome you and we adopt you into the Christ Family, a family of humble souls serving brotherly love and service to God. We are a family of humanitarians. Perhaps you would like to join our family! Remember, no blood test is required, just good deeds!

Sharing?
Amen to that. Can you tell us more about the Holy Grail and the Grail Romances?

Lady Magdalene:
The Grail Romances are quite captivating, and through mystery, they slowly reveal more treasures of truth. I am your treasure of truth, right here, right

now. So, please do not mourn for the loss of any lost memoirs, or any other religious relics.

Parts of my writings were ripped out. (The Book of Mary). So what. I am here now speaking through this messenger, to tell you what is important to focus on. If lost religious relics are found, then bless it as the will of God. However, don't go looking for them.

Also know that there are several acts of channeling in the Holy Bible and in religious documents. So, if someone has told you that New Age channeling is sorcery or evil, remember that many biblical saints and prophets have been accepted as hearing the true voice of God. I am a voice from God Our Father, and the Goddess Our Mother.

My purpose is to bridge everything together, Mother/Father, Sister/Brother, Husband/Wife. My purpose is to see all human relationships connected and streaming with love, knowledge and unity, while sharing experiences back and forth. I am your 'Morningstar Pathfinder' overseeing your Resurrection into Eternal Life. I am your sister and your friend. I am your equal.

Sharing?
We see your vision clearly. It is profoundly beautiful.

How many times will humanity choose to examine the actual *Shroud of Turin* before they finally look within themselves, to the mystery of their own divinity? Some metaphysical seekers see this so clearly!

Lady Magdalene:
Exactly, but do have compassion for all seekers of truth and wisdom, because once they have exhausted the evidence, they will naturally look within. The proof is in the heart. They just need to see that. Remember how many times Jesus used the metaphor of the *Blind Man*.

Jesus is bound to wait for you to go within and transform yourself, before he can meet you. I am assuming that many humans would like to know us?

Sharing?
That is an understatement. Yes.

Lady Magdalene:
Go within, please, because the union you seek can only happen with your participation. Be not stuck in some romanticized fantasy that Heaven will come down for you from some prophesied silver cloud, because you stayed silent in your guilt and apathy waiting for Revelations to happen, in each crucifying detail.

The predicted horrors of The Book of Revelations at will not happen. That probability has been completely changed because humanity has evolved enough in the past forty-six years, to shift everything into love. The completion of The Christ Consciousness Grid* also played into this.

There will be a need for some Earth Changes through earthquakes, to heal the Mother Earth. No nuclear explosions will happen. Those horrible things would set you back drastically in your development.

No more 911* 'acts from lambs'* will have to happen. That incident was contrived by The Dark, so be not ignorant of that fact.

Remember that doing your part may be as simple as spending an hour each day in prayer. The prayers of the world grow every day. This is a blessed planet and you have learned about tough love. Through the fire, you developed deep courage, character, honor and love. Other beings of the universe marvel in the telling of your experience. Your uniquely magnificent, free-will planet is in the limelight.

Just remember that this Grand Procession of God has an invitation list that excludes nobody. So don't exclude yourself, you are most welcome!

Sharing?
We believe your words will greatly impact millions, thank you. We would like to be of service to you.

Lady Magdalene:
You have been with me in service, all along. We have traveled together through this brutal period of time, which has felt like a never-ending tragedy. I thank you all for your courageous service.

Sharing?
We would like your synopsis of *The Holy Grail Legends* and the extreme interest in your life story that resulted from books like *Holy Blood Holy Grail* and *The Da Vinci Code*.

Lady Magdalene:
What makes The Holy Grail real is what you carried from the inside. There is no *Holy Place or thing* on the planet that can replace the deep introspection required to unearth the *divine you* that must birth from within you. However, the stories from our history are sensational.

Ask yourself this; did I dream this belief, or did I believe this dream? That is some potent food for thought regarding the nature of reality. Myths and legends become a catalyst for our growth.

The *placebo effect* of the Mythic Christ French Bloodline proves that instead of a DNA test, you passed the most important test. And you have won the Holy Grail through your noble quest and your clear comprehension of Jesus/ Sananda's true teachings. Just like in the movie "The Da Vinci Code', in the end what really mattered was that Sophie was reconnected with her family. It did not matter to Sauniere that Sophie find the actual sarcophagus of my bones, for proof to the world of whom she was! She found herself when she found her family, and the love is ultimately what mattered. You are humanly divine, and divinely human. Seek to find yourself within.

The Mythic Sara
may we carry her safely into the New Heaven on Earth
let us not misinterpret her true purpose
let us not miscarry her true meaning
for she represents the Mythic Holy Grail
The Christ Child in us all.
Let us forgive the centuries of bloodshed
spilled from the intense dramas of patriarchal rule
Let us shift the theme of Pisces which was sacrifice
to the soft compassion of understanding
Stand up and say no more, to Holy War!
Let us release the complex dramas,
associated with our religious and spiritual beliefs

My Dear Daughters of the Holy Grail
I honor and love you all
and I reincarnated again and again into your families
I was once crucified along side you dear sisters
by the Witches Hammer!
Know that in releasing the deepest pain, we will gain
the most fulfilling FREEDOM!

Oh my Dearest Knights of Light
may no stone lay unturned.
Nothing can hide any longer as the hour of Truth
shines upon us all, dazzling yet frightening for many
Fear not and may the Jewels of your undying devotion
Bless your New Holy Grail Light Body of the New Earth
Let us build The New Heaven my dear supporters
I will always be a part of you,
as you will always be a part of me.
Namaste' my dear Lords and Ladies of The Grail

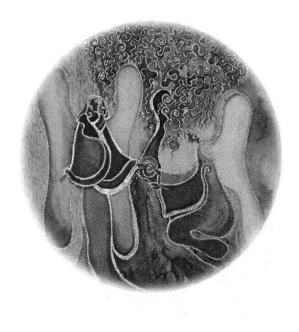

🕯🕯 ✡ **9** ✡ 🕯🕯

John the Baptist
& The Angels

Sharing?
Can you tell us about John the Baptist and what is the Holy Ghost or the Holy Spirit?

Lady Magdalene:
He was a pure, shining star from God! John the Baptist was the spiritual brother of my heart and I loved him dearly. Jesus and I, visited John the Baptist at the river Jordan. The three of us were very close friends.

The Holy Spirit / Holy Ghost is the name of the divine feminine spirit and presence of God. In Hebrew, Sh'kina means "dwelling place" and like Her Tantric counterpart, the Shakti, the Sh'kina was the source of all "soul" in the universe. The Holy Spirit is the feminine aspect of God, who dwells inside every individual, the Goddess Within, the female soul of God.
The Divine Feminine, The Angels and many spiritual guides wait for your command. They wait to do your bidding. They wait for you to learn about co-creating Heaven on Earth with them. It needs to be a group effort.

The Holy Spirit was alive in John the Baptist, Jesus' cousin. John was like the fire of God's wild passion exemplified in a magical wild man, living in nature, unrestrained to societies rules. He was a fine role model to mold Jesus, at that time. Following the transference of The Holy Spirit to Jesus in the river Jordan, Jesus went alone into the desert for forty days, as the Holy Bible states.

The Catholics state this, "In the name of The Father, The Son and The Holy Spirit."

The Father, (God Our Heavenly Father, The Divine Masculine, The Father Aspect of God and The Creator God, Christ Michael, the Father of this local universe.)

The Son (Man is The Son, it is Humanity as a group, and individual humans)

The Holy Spirit (The Shekina, The Divine Feminine. The Mother Aspect of God. Mother Earth's Spirit, also known as Gaia, and all The Angels and spiritual guides.)

Sharing?
Who is Christ Michael? What do you mean by *Christ Michael is the Father of this local universe?*

Lady Magdalene:
He is acting as 'Father' of this local universe. In other words this is a sacred position (job) of the spiritual hierarchy. It is Christ Michael's job to act as the highest liaison with God. He is in the position of the closest contact with the Creator, (Our Heavenly Father).

Sharing?
The Urantia Book says that Jesus Christ was Christ Michael? Can you explain?

Lady Magdalene:
Christ Michael was/is the tutor of Jesus Christ, The Planetary Prince of Peace.
A 'Planetary Prince' is a position (job) of the spiritual hierarchy. The soul of
Jesus was incarnated into the physical body of Jesus. What you may not know is
that Christ Michael incarnated into the same physical body as Jesus. They were
both incarnated into the one physical body. Then after the Resurrection, Christ
Michael returned to Heaven and Jesus did not return, He stayed in the physical
body of Jesus. He had to lower his vibration to be detected by our human eyes.
This is how his apostles were able to see him after the Resurrection.

Sharing?
So the truth is that Christ Michael Ascended to Heaven, and the man, Jesus,
lived on Earth into his senior years so he could be married to you.

Lady Magdalene:
Yes and to continue to minister the people worldwide.

The Angelic Realm

Sharing?
We are fascinating with Angels! What more can you tell us about the Angelic
Realm?

Lady Magdalene:
The Angels is here on Earth with you now to help you adjust to the New World
about to give birth.

Sharing?
Didn't Jesus Christ spend time learning and interacting with the Essenes?

Lady Magdalene:
Yes, and they were *angelologists*, communing with The Angels in prayer, daily.
Jesus spent time in Qumran, on the shores of the Dead Sea with this religious
sect called the Essenes. The Essenes had documented accounts of Jesus' ministry
recorded by different people, written on scrolls that are not in your Holy Bible.
Members of the Essenes also traveled to India with Jesus after his exile from

the Holy Land, after the Resurrection. Scrolls preserved for centuries still exist today and at certain Tibetan monasteries, they protect their sacred knowledge.

Sharing?
How can we commune with The Angels directly to assist us in our healing process?

Lady Magdalene:
I would recommend an I.ET.(Integrated Energy Therapy) healing session* I.E.T. uses the violet angelic energy ray, as brought to the planet through the nine Healing Angels of the Energy Field, to work directly with your 12-Strand Spiritual DNA. I.E.T. supports you in safely and gently releasing limiting energy patterns of your past, empowering and balancing your life in the present, and helps you to reach for the stars as you evolve into your future. Through this powerful therapy The Angels can directly assist you on your healing path.

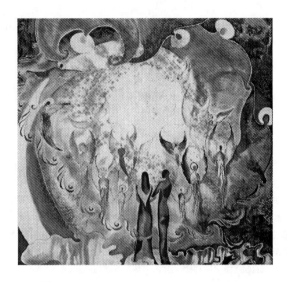

The Angel Matrix

May the Angel Matrix
help you rebuild your dreams,
from the broken pieces of your lost soul,
may you come back together,
with the magical alchemy,
in your ancient perfect DNA,
God's Gifts will be restored to you,
and use them well,
Shatter hell,
for the illusion that it was,
yet now gone.
Be The Angel Matrix, with The Angels,
be the
Human Angels Helping Human Kind.

10

Rewiring of the human body's circuitry

Sharing?
Can you comment on the *Virgin Birth*?

Lady Magdalene:
That is an excellent question. Yes, Mother Mary did have a Virgin Conception. But the term 'virgin' should not be confused with the Dogma of *virginity equals divine perfection, or sanctification.* That is a religious myth.

The physical reason for a 'Virgin Birth' was to create a Messiah that would be seeded not from a human man, of that time, because of a Damaged God Connection. The physical body of every person in those times was damaged, or disabled, in a way that has to do with The Divine Connection to God. Before *The Fall* this severed God connection did not exist; that was Original Innocence.

The physical way a Damaged God Connection happens is through the bodies severed energy circuitry. It is like being rewired to not operate correctly. This was a deliberate act, by the Dark Anti-evolutionary Forces, intending to harm and enslave humanity.

For women this severed connection caused a disconnection from their center of power. For men this severed connection caused a disconnection from their emotional center. Thus, anti-evolutionary forces planted the seeds of the *Battle of the Sexes.* Ancient humans of the body of God's government were tricked by these anti-evolutionary forces, to agreed, (on the other side of the veil we voted) to this rewiring of the human energy circuitry.

Sharing?
Do you mean to say that the human brain and DNA was rewired like reprogramming a computer?

Lady Magdalene:
Yes and the females were rewired differently then the men. So now is the time for women to become 'empowered' and for men to connect back to 'the heart'. We can heal the damage and become whole again. The 12 stand DNA will be restored in you!

Sharing?
So the genetics of Christ, through the *Virgin Conception* of Mary, was perfect and undamaged, thus allowing him to perform miracles?

Lady Magdalene:
Yes, although he did indeed work hard to develop his gifts. Also, know that for Christ to be 'gifted' in this way carried with it a huge burden of responsibility. Christ's mission had to be successful.

God had a plan. Immortal spiritual beings, (called the Tat Brotherhood) sanctified by God, working with The Christ Group, knowing that our bodies had this severed God connection, implemented God's plan of a 'Virgin Birth'. This was planned, hundreds of years in advance. The success of Christ's mission was astronomically important. Saving Planet Earth has required that certain things take place, which most people don't fully understand. God's so called 'mysterious ways', or the use of rituals, when used for saving your planet, should never be judged.

The spiritual power of The Christ Group* was very real. Just know that what you never understood about Mother Mary's Virgin Birth, was kept from you, until the appropriate time would come for you to understand it. The creation of the baby Jesus did not occur through normal sexual intercourse. The love ritual that created Jesus with the involvement of the Angel Gabriel was necessary, for the Power of God to work through him. Know that 'the way' in which Jesus was conceived was only allowed for that purpose. Mother Mary and Joseph went on to have many more children, the normal way, through sexual intercourse. Do you see?

Think of it like this, to have a Christ with a severed God connection, well this would be quite a gamble. On the other hand, sending a Christ that did not have a severed God connection, well, this would stand a better chance of succeeding. The Holy Genetics of Christ's Bloodline has preserved an example of genetic divine potential. The enhanced psychic and telepathic abilities of the Holy Bloodline of Christ will soon be revealed as more of this lineage learns of their heritage. However, please know that these same abilities can be learned by anyone with the sincere intent to develop them. The Christ Bloodline has a genetic advantage, creating a natural ability. They are gifted. After the Ascension everyone's gifts and Divine connection will be restored, so very soon, none of this 'Jesus Christ Bloodline sensation' will matter at all.

There are Sacred Geometry and many Sacred Metaphysical Sciences that are far beyond your current awareness. Spiritual Power or magic through alchemy takes a lot of maturity to handle. The abuse of these types of powers is evident in the *Fall of Atlantis*. Heaven's technology would blow you away! However, with great power there comes great responsibility.

11

Heaven's Technology

Sharing?
Heaven's technologies, I like the sound of that. Do these technologies work in harmony with nature?

Lady Magdalene:
Absolutely, Yes! Man has disregarded nature and raped her. Technology should work in harmony with ecology and nature. Heaven's technologies can heal this world's environmental problems. Heaven's technologies and Love can heal all the worlds' problems! First, you must be mature enough though, as to not abuse powerful tools.

When all humans on the planet show care and compassion to each other fully and unconditionally, you will fully utilize these gifts from God. Many gifts from God have been withheld from you by the Dark ones in power. The time is coming to let them out of hiding. These treasures are great, so rejoice!

Sharing?
Yes, indeed. And bombs to kill will become extinct here, yes! That is our idea of Heaven on Earth. Does the Mother Ship as described in the book *The Crystal Stair, A Guide to The Ascension*, really exist?

Lady Magdalene:
Yes it does, and just as it is described in that book. I miss not being there with you know whom.

Sharing?
You are funny Lady Magdalene. Where are you Lady Magdalene, if not with your eternal husband Jesus?

Lady Magdalene:
Doing Lightwork, abroad. I am spread out into different dimensional beings, not limited to just one form and one life. I can better serve my purpose this way. My higher self and soul directs the process. So, understand that as I speak to you now, I am also living many lives and we are all multi dimensional beings with this capacity.

I was never the '*sit on a cloud and eat marshmallow pies with cupids*', kind of angel helper. Direct experience on the planet works best. So, although I do reside in the higher realms, I am also in the 3rd dimension, living certain lives for the purpose of creating a bridge of clear understanding and compassion. I know your difficulties and emotional pain through my own experiences.

I am also clearing out the rest of my own emotional pain, from traumas that I experienced in certain lives. It is a lightening to release and heal these buried hurts and have the heaviness lift off of one's energy field. I am clearing out any residual guilt or shame that I housed within myself, from many lives on Earth.

Know this; you will succeed in ascending to your soul and to God, after you clear out that which does not serve you. It should be as natural as taking your next breath. Although I do know how hard it can be to '*release*' and '*let go*' in the 3rd dimension.

Sharing?
Can you comment of what is called unity consciousness?

Lady Magdalene:
All fear lives in the energy of separation.
All joy lives in the energy of union.

The Dark had a reason for assassinating people like Bob Marley and Lady Diana. The two that I mention, both had the potential to start movements so huge, that they could have shifted the entire planet into a much higher frequency of Love and Light. They did do this in their lives but had they not been assassinated; they could have potentially created the unity that would have triggered 'critical mass' for Planetary Ascension to occur.

Sound healing* can help groups achieve unity. If the music speaks from the heart, then it does not matter what genre of music it is. Rock music has sometimes blasted us into a higher way of thinking. That can be appropriate. Soft new age music soothes the soul. That can be appropriate. The rap music of Lauryn Hill, exposes the truth of human suffering. That can be appropriate. If it raises consciousness for healing it is of The Light.

Sharing?
We have read on the internet that Jesus rejects rock music and says it is detrimental to achieving a higher state of consciousness. We believe that the rock band U2 creates unity. Can you comment on that?

Lady Magdalene:
Yes, *The Dark* would want you to believe that all rock music is very discordant and is detrimental to raising consciousness. On the contrary, some rock music does open hearts and minds, to in turn, raise consciousness. The music of the sixties is a good example. The rock of the sixties raised our consciousness, in a blasting way. Do you see?

Sharing?
Yes, but many fell into drug addiction.

Lady Magdalene:
This is true and that was a negative by-product of that era. But humanity learned about drug abuse, and its negative consequences. Mistakes help us learn and grow.

There is a lesson in being nonjudgmental in regards to the like and dislikes of other people. Respect the likes and dislikes of different types of people. Judge not, another's way.

Sharing?
What tools or ways of transformation and healing would you recommend?

Lady Magdalene:
Connect with Angelic Healers and ones working with the *Et Healers* as well. Crystals, nature hikes, sunshine, all types of meditation, prayer and any form of emotional body healing, sound healing and many other forms of healing are available. If your intent is strong enough, sometimes, you don't ever need tools, because the real reason a tool works in because you are effectively using your intent!

Sharing?
The Crucifix, does this graven image upset you?

Lady Magdalene:
Thank you so much for mentioning that. I would love it, if everyone would be willing to put their *Crucifix* away, lay it to rest and lock it in the vaults of yesterday. He is not suffering, and as for the suffering he did go through, it has been emotionally released, so very long ago. It happened between his crucifixion and his resurrection. That was 2000 years ago. Mourn not, for he says, rejoice!

Sharing?
I wish the Holy Land could hear that right now! Suffer generators, we have become a planet of suffer generators! We want that to change. How fast can it change?

Lady Magdalene:
Literally, over night, but most humans need things to happen slowly and gracefully. Slower beings need to bud in their correct timing. Severe quick change is too harsh for many. It's like waiting for the fledgling bird to catch up with the flock. It takes utmost compassion to not exclude anyone. It's like the firefighter going into the burning house for the kitten. God excludes no one, just like the heroic firefighter. The Book of Revelation, a method of prediction, is being altered by your good works every day! The heavy drama of the transition is now predicted to be tolerable for the most part.

Sharing?
'Heaven on Earth' is emerging by our good works. That's good news. Can you comment on the part of Revelations stating that we will reign with Christ for 1000 years?

Lady Magdalene:
Christ will reign here, yes. This reign does not necessarily mean that there will be a 3rd dimensional place for this reign. A spiritual 5th Dimensional Earth world would be closer to the truth.

Sharing?
We are relieved, and comforted by all that you have shared with us. Thank you.

Lady Magdalene:
If nobody told you the game changed with the awesome success of the Christ Grid*, it is understandable that you would be astonished. The Christ Grid * and the awesome work of many Lightworkers have helped this planet's coming transition. The Incubator Effect has worked well and now The Birth of the New Earth is proceeding without complications.

Sharing?
So, because it is not predestined that Revelations would happen verbatim, then why was it written? Just to scare us silly?

Lady Magdalene:
Some of you are still scared silly! The Book of Revelation was written to warn you of what can happen, if humanity followed on a certain path. You have changed that path. The battle of the old and the new energy is still playing out though, in a *tug of war*. Know this. The victory for the Light is secure. There will still be some drama, but stand tall in your faith in us.

Disaster preparedness I would recommend, but just get together a few weeks of supplies and do not move into fear.

Do question governmental authority. God is watching and The Mother Ship and many fleets of ships are near, and ready to help humanity. However, they are there mostly as a safety precaution. They will not interfere unless it is an emergency situation and absolutely necessary.

Know that God's entourage has many surprises in a store for you. Political upheaval is right on the horizon. Truth is unfolding every day, and on a foundation of truth, you will rebuild this world. Healing on all levels will happen.

Enormous political uprising is on the horizon. The propaganda machine and the falseness of the media will soon be exposed. The world is going to get rocky so hold on to your seats and expect severe change that will lead to the rebuilding of your world.

Visualize what you want and it will be. Know that the need for ongoing war was never necessary. You have been led to believe in war. War kills innocent people, what is good about that? The motives and agendas of politics and profits are no excuse for killing innocent people, in any part of the world!

Sharing?
So when will Jesus come back?

Lady Magdalene:
Christ will come back very soon, (years not decades, but potentially it can happen any time now) with the beings of the Great White Brotherhood*, the Spiritual Hierarchy*, and all of the Heavenly Hosts*. Many star people from other galaxies are also here to help mankind.

However, you should know that the point is to bring Heaven '*down to earth*'. You are the 'grounding crew'* If Jesus were to come down with the whole group now, it would disrupt the awakening process of those people not quite ready to ascend. So the Planet Earth, our Mother Gaia is holding off for as long as she can. Her Earthquakes are a part of the Ascension process.

Our hope is that all people on Earth will be able to stay in the fourth dimension, after the Great Shift. If a person does not let go of fear, they will probably not be able to stay in that dimension. If you make it, by holding your focus in Love and Light, then the Master Jesus will be meeting '*the you*' that will be a fourth dimensional you.

In this new magical dimension, you will be trained in handling the instant manifestations. You see, in this *New Heaven* that will be *Earth Ascended* you can think anything and it will appear immediately. If you fear that the enemies are out to get you, then that thought will manifest instantly into your reality. The twin to this awesome power will be responsibly. If you cannot handle controlling your thoughts, you will be bumped back down into a lower dimensional place.

Sharing?
So there will be two Earths, a 3rd dimensional Earth and a 4th dimensional Earth?

There will be the relocating of the ones not able to sustain higher states of consciousness. The overpopulation problem of planet Earth will be corrected. The pollution of the planet is horrendous and Mother Earth can no longer sustain her life in this pollution. The *Celestials* will be clearing out our air pollution with their divine technology.

Know that the relocated ones will be placed where they can continue to evolve. Life is a learning process and a planet like a school enrolls the appropriate students for that school. Your vibration or level of mastery will need to match where you are placed. If you are not ready to stay in a higher frequency planet earth, due to your vibration, then you may be relocating. Remember that in your schools, lessons can be repeated. Opportunities for growth are endless in all the Universes. The intention is for every single human to embrace God and Ascend!

🕯🕯 ✡ 12 ✡ 🕯🕯

The Lady Nada Becomes The Goddess Isis

Sharing?
Can you tell us about any other lives that you have lived, here on planet Earth?

Lady Magdalene:
Yes. It is a joy to share with you. I was the Goddess Isis. However, that significant life should not be over glamorized. I was just doing the job that God gave me to do. Every woman is a Goddess, as every man is also a God. When one aligns with their *Divine Purpose*, then *Divinity* becomes who you are!

My life as the Goddess Isis created my qualification, to be a part of The Christ Group*, the ones responsible for overseeing the Resurrection of Christ. The Christ Group*, had a specific plan to follow. You must understand that twin souls usually work together. I was excited to be a part of my twin soul's mission to be The Messiah.

Sharing?
'The Goddess in The Gospels', as you are called by the author Margaret Starbird, gives the clue that you were very connected to The Mother Goddess Isis. You were trained in the ways of The Goddess in Avalon. Were they aware of this Isis connection?

Lady Magdalene:
Yes, and they worked with The Christ Group*. They knew of my sacred reincarnation as the returning Goddess Isis. The Druids and High Priestesses were quite aware of reincarnation. So now, you can probably understand that as the reincarnated Isis, I had quite a well-established resume for my job. God is an excellent administrator!

Now, what you do not know about me as the Goddess Isis, is that I actually came from Atlantis. In Atlantis, I was known as the High Priestess Lady Nada. I was an artist as well and I designed beautiful temples of crystal and glass. The sacred beauty of Atlantis was all destroyed when the Dark Force's abuse of sacred power, escalated to the demise of the entire civilization. The entire continent sank into the ocean.

The misuse of the Crystal Power caused the need for ending The Golden Age of Atlantis. It was very sad. The saddest part was the *Magnetic Erasure*, caused by the poles shifting. That caused humans to revert back to a *cave man mentality*. They lost their memories. They were lowered in vibration. The ones who escaped Atlantis right before the collapse, left with their high technology and spiritual knowledge, to colonize in other parts of the world. The one you know as Osiris also left Atlantis with our group. Our new home became Egypt. In Egypt I became known as Isis.

Now when Isis and Osiris showed up in Egypt with their 'magic', which was their technology and sacred knowledge, they were worshiped by the people as Gods. Isis taught these simple people about mothering and homemaking. Our technology from Atlantis must have made us look like Gods. The worship of higher beings? Remember we are all equals!

Sharing?
That is incredible. We have heard before that Lady Nada was Jesus' twin flame, but we did not know that Lady Nada was also Isis.

Lady Magdalene:
Yes, so through prophecies, the priestesses of Avalon knew I was the reincarnated Isis.

Sharing?
There is a movie called *The Mists of Avalon* that portrays the King Arthur story and the Legends of Camelot, Avalon, and Celtic Christianity? Does this movie tell the truth about those times?

Lady Magdalene:
The movie is entirely true and the story is well told. It eloquently portrays the human drama's that important spiritual figures in history have gone through.

All humans here have these same human dramas. They are the learning ground and preparation for the Ascension process, which is for all to experience.

Sharing?
So you were quite prepared before you met Jesus, to be a big part of his ministry, and his closest disciple and lover?

Lady Magdalene:
Absolutely! However, the spiritual training I had was not shelter from the brutality of the times and the emotional scares that resulted from that brutality. I was very much human and so was Christ. But, his love poured out with so much intensity and pure heartedness that being around him was electrifying. And imagine how much more the feeling was for myself, being that we were in love. Wow, that still gives me chills to think about!

Sharing?
Chills and Goose bumps from us too!

Lady Magdalene:
I am blushing. (smiles)

Sharing?
Was it strange being the only female apostle?

Lady Magdalene:
Strange, indeed. I was certainty boisterous enough to handle it. Yet on the outside I was very quiet. Jesus knew the real me.
I have been called the first apostle, by some of your modern authors. I was in actuality the first apostle that Jesus got to know, because it all started when the Roman Centurion and I, initiated his ministry in the Holy Land.

Each one of the apostles represented an archetype, or aspect of human nature. Each one served a purpose. My purpose was to be hidden. Now the time has come for my purposes to be revealed. As the 13th Apostle* I embodied the archetype of the myth of evil, the '*judged one*'.

The natural 13th month calendar year was also hidden from you. The true calendar, know as the Mayan Calendar, would set humans back into the natural rhythms of nature. With the 13th Month Calendar concealed, we have lived out of the natural flow of nature. Accusing healers working with nature and herbs, as evil, also relates to the cursed number 13. It a magical number, yes, but it is not evil.

Sharing?
Fascinating. We know of the Mayan Calender you speak of. As the Bible says there is a time for everything, and we see how your detachment from judgment is just a deeper understanding.

Lady Magdalene:
Thank you. I am so glad you got it! Just know that the best is yet to come. Your connection to your Creator will be repaired, and women and men can be powerful together! Men and women are healing the issues that came about from the *Battle of the Sexes*. The reuniting with your Twin Flame* is very joyful.

Sharing?
The thought of this is exciting! This gift of the Twin Soul*, does this explain our obsession with romantic love?

Lady Magdalene:
Yes it does. You are not silly romantic dreamers, girls! You do have a perfect male counterpart, and he will be able to feel you, and support your empowerment.

Sharing?
That is beautiful!

13

The Magdalene Returns as Sister Aimee

Sharing?
Do you have any other important past lives, to share with us?

Lady Magdalene:
Yes, I do. If you look at it in a linear fashion, Sister Aimee Semple McPherson was actually my future life.

I was Sister Aimee Semple McPherson, born in Ontario Canada, in 1890. My mother in that life, was one of the founders of the Salvation Army. I was raised Pentecostal, and amongst gospel singers. The darkness of the reign of Hitler was approaching and I was consecrated by God to become a Faith Healer.

My Greatest Love, Jesus, worked with me, from the other side of *The Veil*, to heal thousands of people at tent revivals and Church services. I built and dedicated the Angelus Temple in Los Angeles in 1923. Millions of people attended services there, in my ministry years.

The life I lived as Sister Aimee Semple McPherson is well documented.

Sharing?
That's incredible. You preformed literal prayer healings with Jesus. Is there a biography about her that we can read?

Lady Magdalene:
Yes, the book called *Sister Aimee*, by Daniel Mark Epstein tells the story well. The challenge for me as Aimee would come when I was a newlywed in China. I married Robert Semple, an evangelist, at the young age of seventeen. He died from food poisoning while we were serving as missionaries in China. The year

was 1911 and I was returning to the states alone and brokenhearted with my newborn baby. Years after that, I experienced physical illness that was the catalyst for my growth, which led me to embrace my divine calling in that life.

Sharing?
We are beginning to see the Mary Magdalene correlation here. You had to pick up your role as a spiritual leader, the part of your Mission that could not manifest in The Holy Land?

Lady Magdalene:
Yes and I did have a loving mother to guide me. She was my reflection of strength. She had a big heart, like Jesus' Mother Mary.

The challenge and the accomplishment for me, as Aimee was to rise above my health and emotional issues with the pure courage to surrender to the will of The Father and His Plan for me, and it did happen. I became an Ascended Master through my deeds in that life.

To clarify something right now you must know that every time I refer to God as male or as The Father, I also carry knowledge and love for the majesty of The Mother Aspect of God, The Divine Feminine and the Mother Earth. I was never patriarchal in my thinking.

As Sister Aimee I was Trinitarian, meaning God the Father*, The Son* and the Holy Spirit (Holy Ghost)*. However, the ways of church dogma and 'fundamentalism' was not really a part of Aimee's soul, but it was part of those times? Do you see? You live what you learn from your family and community. The important part of my life as Aimee was my success in faith healing, through the Holy Spirit and my twinsoul Jesus. This gave clear proof to the miracles of healing that can happen with a strong and clear connection to God.

Sharing?
Wow. That is awesome. So are you a Pentecostal Christian now?

Lady Magdalene:
Well I prefer to be known as nondenominational, with a respect for all denominations that promote the direct experience of God, by going within oneself.

Now as Aimee I was very charismatic and headstrong so leadership became easy to me in that life. My personality was appropriate for my job. However, the price of fame is a lack of privacy, which can become out of balance. The worship of idols? Hummm, that can be a dangerous thing.

My spirit truly did soar to the Heavens as I unknowingly preached about my eternal husband and his teachings. As united twin souls, we healed thousands, (Jesus and I). The healings were called prayer healing or faith healing. Certain irreverent critics thought that the healing services I held were far too spectacular. Well, too bad for them, that they cannot enjoy God and absorb His gifts more fully. The sick and the poor loved me and I just flowed with it. The congregations became huge.

Sharing?
Thank you for this introduction of such a fascinating life that you lived. God honored your desires to be united with your love, and heal thousands through your love and connection with Jesus, God and The Holy Spirit!

Lady Magdalene:
Can you see now, how it's no sacrifice at all, that I had severe suffering in so many different lives? The earned blessings are endless, like the moons, planets, stars, and unlimited childlike joy and abundance of the Universe.

Sharing?
Yes, we are feeling that fullness now. We honor you and yet we promise we won't idolize you.

Lady Magdalene:
Thank you.
Be like little children. The Kingdom of God is fast approaching. Be ready in your heart to receive many gifts. Nurture your Holy Chalice* like a mother shelters her babes. Be happy. Be Content. God loves you and is revealed to you, as you heal and open yourselves. God is like looking into the eyes of a little baby. The unconditional love can be felt and in the innocence of the experience, God is saying, "I am bound to you, as you are to me; feed me with your closeness, let me in!" Let God in.

Sharing?
Wow, so the intensity of *Divine Love* needs our big willingness to be extremely open and forgiving, like a child?

Lady Magdalene:
Yes! And, please forgive God because God is aware of your rejection. He/She is a loving parent and wants the best for you. Your smiles are The Creator's smiles

Sharing?
I have read about Sister Aimee's passionate portrayals of The Crucifixion/ Resurrection during church services. Did you know you were portraying your own past life experience?

Lady Magdalene:
On a consciousness level no, but it sure explains why I was so moved and emotional in playing out the drama. (smiles)

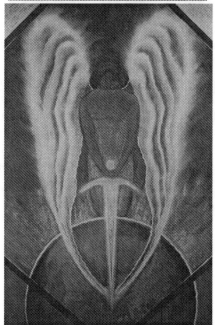

Got Michael?
Twin Flames, Lady Faith & Archangel Michael

☪ ☪ ✡ **14** ✡ ☪ ☪

The Pen is a
Mighty Sword

Lady Magdalene:
The crucifying wounds of war are not going to stop until every human stands up for peace! The major point that most people miss is that every human must now wake up and know that Christ asks you to be the rebel and protest the current fake government. The ones in control use their power for profit, with complete disregard for human life. This must stop and you need to shout it out in every way you can! The pen is a mighty sword and peaceful war protests are effective as well. Get involved now!

Sharing?
Do you have prophecies to share with us Lady Magdalene?

Lady Magdalene:
There will be earthquakes and political upheaval. The old ways must crumble apart to make way for the new. This is an unavoidable fact. It is part of the cleansing process that the Earth and her inhabitants will be going through. Do not move into fear. However, if you live on the California coastline I suggest that you move once it is publicly announced that earthquakes are coming to the area. A televised warning from Christ may precede the Earth Changes, and you will be instructed on how to protect yourselves.

Sharing?
Is this prediction avoidable?

Lady Magdalene:
Absolutely! Just like always, with enough prayer and right action, prophecies can be completely altered.

Just know that the Birth of the New Earth is so close. Just a few more pushes! Those pushes will look like crazy behavior to many people still in the dark. They will hopefully come to an understanding that the will of God is upon them and this cannot be ignored.

Sharing?
Were references to reincarnation edited from the Christian Bible?

Lady Magdalene:
Yes, they were. You need to know that The Buddha and Christ are united on the Other Side of The Veil. These two Ascended Masters would both tell you that the need to reincarnate repeatedly, is ended through Mastery and Ascension. The act of Karma Clearing is demonstrated in the rituals of the early Christians. This is linked to the ancient knowledge that Jesus absorbed through his travels in the Himalayas and with his close association with the Essenes.

Jesus taught that ancient knowledge (gnosis) combined with Faith Healing brought us home to God. Prayer that is inspired by deep feeling has so much power! It truly is the strength of your intention and the depth of your love that really moves the mountains. The doubting Thomas types are still looking for the proof of how the mountain moves. It moves with your powerful and passionate faith and intent!

Sharing?
What else do Christ and the Buddha advocate from the other side?

Lady Magdalene:
Deep Forgiveness. The Buddhists believe that through 'reincarnation', their spiritual leader Buddha is reincarnated through the Dali Lama. The Dali Lama's most important message 'forgiveness', is one of Jesus Christ's most important messages to you also. Through Buddha and Christ, we need to learn that forgiving our enemy has the potential to transform our enemy, thus restoring understanding and Peace on Earth. Your supposed enemy may be your sister, brother or it could be that a friend has stabbed you in the back. Usually we are our own worst enemy, so it is most important to forgive and love yourself!

Nations at war with each other should use radical forgiveness, to heal all the damage.

Sharing?
When the heart of a nation is black, and that nation has controlled, manipulated, and murdered its own people for so long, how *in the world* are they ever going to see the errors of their ways?

Lady Magdalene:
Perhaps they will seek and ask for forgiveness. Woe to those who do not seek redemption! Usually it is the leaders of nations, that are black and the nation's people suffer as a result of that. Know that, if there were ever a time to stand up to the power-abusers, it is now!

Remember that hate stems from the paradigm that the only way to stop your enemy from killing you, is to kill back. Envy and jealousy stems from the paradigm that there is not enough for everyone, thus resulting in Material Elitism, (*hoarding of riches*) and Spiritual Elitism, (*Your path is wrong. Therefore, you are not worthy of God's forgiveness and redemption*).

The truth is, God has enough love and abundance for every human on the planet. The challenge is to be like God, and have overflowing love and generosity in your own heart. All races, religions and cultures should be cherished. Can you love all of the races, religions and cultures of humankind, with undying faith and forgiveness? Remember what Jesus said. You are your brother's keeper.

Sharing?
What should we expect from Jesus? Everybody knows the phrase here, 'Jesus is coming and boy is he pissed!' Really, we just want to know what he is like.

Lady Magdalene:
Well, he is not pissed, but he will tell you the truths about what changes need to be made in your world. He will be coming back to set the records straight with all of the Christian churches, about what he really did teach 2000 years ago. So the distortions of what he taught will clear. He will withdraw his Holy Presence from the churches that choose to ignore him. The understanding of reincarnation was a part of his original teachings.

All of your incarnations have made you who you are today. Life is a continuance and life is eternal. Leaving parts out of the picture causes a break in the flow of understanding ones whole being. Holistic thinking is needed, do you see?

Sharing?
Yes we do, and we embrace reincarnation!

Lady Magdalene
This is great, that you already understand. Perhaps you can help other understand this. Through propaganda, churches created the idea that you die and go to Heaven or Hell, and the Hell bound ones have no other chance for redemption. This thinking is simple wrong. It is this belief that has allowed *The Dark* to control you through fear. If you really want to honor Christ, get involved in educating people about this fact. Also, get involved with humanitarian projects. What ideas do you have? There is plenty of work to be done in many areas. Find your unique specialty.

If you want to be united in Christ's true teachings then you will need to release your misconceptions about his teachings. Churches have led you astray.

Please don't call him God, and do not bow. He dislikes humanity putting him on a pedestal. The best way to honor him is to honor your own sense of divinity. He and I wish to inspire you to reach in and bring that beautiful soul out! Then in the energy of equality, Jesus/Sananda would love to share with you. Then he will inspire you to be the best you can be, just like a true friend would.

Sharing?
That is enlightening. Our next question is, does your cleared karma make you an Ascended Master, or is this just offered to a select group of highly incredible souls, like yourself and Jesus/Sananda?

Lady Magdalene:
I am so glad you asked that. The answer to the first part of your question is yes. A certain percentage of your Karma needs to be cleared to become an *Ascended Being*. What makes you an ascended being is the quality of your love and compassion. This is not an elitist club! God says *mastership* is for every soul, and we are drawn to our spiritual mastery naturally. It is the magnetic pull of God's divine love and grace that beckons us on and puzzles us too, at times. Then we look for answers within.

Jesus said, 'You will do things greater than I have'. Did he not?

Sharing?
Yes, he did. Nevertheless, many have put him on a pedestal.

Lady Magdalene;
This is true because humankind created Spiritual Elitism, and out of an insecure sense of self, they have run in circles trying to find God outside of themselves. This only makes the one on the pedestal, very lonely.

Sharing?
Yes it does. In regards to the powerful Political Elitism, rumor has it that President Bush's own psychotherapist fears for this country. Can you comment on that?

Lady Magdalene:
When Elitists obtain riches from the blood of someone's suffering, it becomes a thing of darkness. *The Ring of Power* then leaves the soul spellbound and empty. It wants more, like a hungry animal. Does that sound like the ego, greed, and power-hungry insanity problem, of your modern political leaders?

Now do you see that your world is at an all-time high, of imbalances. The creation of poverty through greedy, power hungry leaders also correlates to the deliberate use of religion to propagate the myth of Spiritual Elitism. Currently your institutions are in need of a major clearing of past Karma. The *Ring of Power*, has taught us well. The end is near, and it is time to toss that 'Ring' into the 'vaults of yesterday'.

Sharing?
Lock it up tight! Amen! And may The Holy Land heal to clear the way for a New Jerusalem! We would love to see that happen in our lifetime.

Lady Magdalene:
It is your job to help it birth and it will happen in your lifetimes. This is the time of the Great Awakening! Rejoice!

Sharing?
We are refreshed by your messages, and with renewed hope, we are glad to be in service with you. The soul of the Celtic Christian People, we see this in you Lady Magdalene, can you comment?

Lady Magdalene:
The good Celtic Christian People absorbed the true Jesus and especially the courage and honor part of Christ's teachings. It's like the soul energy of the gypsy with no country, or the king who has no throne, that appeals to me. It's the beauty of migrating birds, or the warm sun shining on your naked back. It is about the love of freedom and individuality, which you recognize in me as Celtic.

All paths to God should be cherished, but naturally, you will have a preference. My preference would be to enlighten all to the beauty of Truth that lives in us all, through our spiritually diverse roots.

As Mary Magdalene I was a High Temple Priestess, but my soul roots were Jewish (from Venus). As Isis, I was the representation of the Mother Goddess for the people. As Sister Aimee Semple McPhersen I was born Pentecostal and I sang gospel songs with a very spirited group. In a few other lives, I was a gypsy, an American Indian woman, an Asian woman and an earth medicine healer woman, burned at the stake. The passionate gravitate together and I have played many dramatic parts, interacting with my brothers and sisters.

To put a religious denominational name to myself does not fit, so you can call me nondenominational if you wish. I wish to embrace and reach everyone.

Sharing?
Was the Book of Mary*, your lost gospel written by yourself? Was The Book of Mary ever stolen and if so, by whom? Can you translate The Book of Mary for us?

Lady Magdalene:
Yes, I was the author of The Book of Mary. The original and whole Book of Mary was stolen from The Roman Centurion, back when Jesus first gave him my gospel, right about the time Christ and the Christ Group* were soon to journey to India.

You see, Jesus knew about the Hall of Records, with the opening at the right paw of the Sphinx. When the Roman Centurion was sent there to archive certain scrolls, he was about to enter the Hall of Records through the paw of the Sphinx and he was attacked and robbed from behind. Who was the thief? I cannot tell you.

I wrote The Book of Mary, to record what was said between Jesus, the apostles and myself, after the Resurrection. He clearly speaks to your soul to awaken you. Jesus gives reference to me seeing him in the fifth dimension, in his Light Body, (I saw him with my spiritual vision and not with my physical eyes) passages 8, 9, 10 and 11. This was true, I did have this vision and Jesus was in his Light Body.

I am clearly the one whom he truly loved unconditionally, and with much dignity and respect. Jesus invented the Women's Liberation Movement, in having me be one of his Apostles. Jesus was showing you that women can be spiritual leaders too.

Sharing?
Amen to that! Can you tell us about what is contained on the missing pages?

Lady Magdalene:
No, I cannot. Perhaps the editor's of my gospel would like an opportunity to bring that information forth?

The religions that appear to be crumbling to the ground can regroup with the acknowledgment of hidden truths. Why not wish the supposed 'enemy', the grace of God's whole forgiveness and clearing of Karma or Clearing of Sin (error) as others call it. Remember leaders need forgiveness too!

Sharing?
In a children's movie, "The Never-ending Story", the hero child has one wish left to save Fantasia. He wishes that the evil queen will begin to feel and get a heart, and it works. Fantasia was restored, because the magic wish was granted and the Queen got a heart, and the evil spell was broken. Does this correlate well, to what you are getting at?

Lady Magdalene:
Yes, you are a brilliant group, I might add! Now do you see the magic of 'love thy enemy'? The enemy is a part of the whole and a part of God. We all have enemies within, as well. Our outer enemies are the mirror images of our inner enemies. When we chose to release our enemies through forgiveness, then they can no longer hurt us. We are then free! Evil will run from you once you claim your power. Believe me. It works.

We all are a part of the never-ending story of God's expanding, infinite creative play. Be like the little child. Be playful. Love. Be in love. Love conquers all.

Sharing?
And All You Need is Love,
Love is All You Need,
from the apostles, John, Paul, George & Ringo

Lady Magdalene:
That's great. Yes, love is the key.

Sharing?
This question comes from one of the members of this group. She says how can anyone forgive the suppressive Catholic Church, a church that ruthlessly crucified millions of woman healers, like yourself? Or how can The Jews ever forgive Hitler for sending millions or people to the concentration camp to be gassed to death. How can it ever be safe enough to be that forgiving?

Lady Magdalene:
I feel you and I have been there, stuck in a quagmire of resentment. However, the cycle of grief should end, and if you are stuck in anger, resentment and righteous indignation, you are only punishing and condemning yourself. Be brave enough to love and forgive repeatedly.

Also, know that the darkest evil ones of this planet are currently being expelled from the planet. You need not fear them any longer.

If we blame and become cold hearted, this will not work. When love is pain, it can devour you. Nevertheless, how can we hold on to that pain and not admit responsibility for the stickiness of the hatred we choose to feed it with. Look for healing through letting go.

I was there once, as Mary Magdalene, convinced that some of the Apostles hated me. When my own people almost stoned me to death, I became caught in a web of cruelty. I have forgiven it all. The drama and trauma, I have fully released. Free your soul through forgiveness. There is much good work to do.

Sharing?
So many Lightworkers are too tired and emotionally broken and in financial stress from serving Spirit through volunteer endeavors. The severity of these problems has led some to completely withdrawal from service. How can they find new hope?

Lady Magdalene:
In your times, you have great information highways! With the internet, film, television, and telephones you can do a lot of rabble-rousing and work to bring about social, political and religious change. Be in the NOW! Don't look back! Lightworkers can be voted into political positions of power. Take political action. The pen is a mighty sword, so swing it like Archangel Michael.

You can be boisterous, outspoken and radical. Christ was lovingly called by the Essenes *The Wicked Priest* because he was a radical rebel. Know that the time is now, to turn over tables like Christ did as the moneychangers dishonored the Holy Temple. This planet is yours, take it back! We realize that you are in financial stress and The Ascension will soon relieve that stress, soon enough. Trust me. It's just around the corner.

Lightwork is hard, slow and painful at times, but so is anything that is really worth it. Be tenacious. It will be worth it. Don't give with resentments attached. Regroup your life to maximize joy, don't play the Atlas. When is the last time you tried to have a party? That long … hummm? Better add some joy!

Sharing?
We hear you. Make love, not bad thoughts, which is *war in the mind*.

Lady Magdalene:
And hell lives in the mind. This is true. This War in The Mind*, then perpetuates, which in turn finds a '*mirror*' in the outside world. The war in the mind, *your mind*, that is the way the anti-christs will win you over to their side. Don't buy it. Stay at peace in your mind. Think with your big heart and growing compassion.

Sharing?
Hell is the nightmare of this planet, that we collectively and individually created.

Lady Magdalene:
Yes, But this dream-spell is changing because humans are awakening.

Sharing?
Parasitic energies are sucking the lifeblood out of every good human in these times. Rising poverty levels, new diseases and governmental fear tactics plaque our thoughts and actions. The complete breakdown of society and even the threat of world war or Marshall Law comes to mind. How can we deal with this?

Lady Magdalene:
By staying light about it, and by getting passionate about changing it. That is kind of a paradox, I know. But you will need to know how to keep everything in balance in the days to come. I created a spiritual tool called The Holon of Balance* to help with this. To create a Holon of Balance, simple visualize two, four-sided pyramids. Now the two, four-sided bases of each pyramid come together, so one pyramid is facing downward and the other one is facing upward. Visualize the person or situation that is traumatized, or hurt or stressed, in the middle of the two pyramids. Also, visualize the Violet Light* engulfing the situation or person. The person can be you, or anyone in need of balance and peace.

It is my purpose to give you courage, strength and faith that fighting in this battle will be worth it. You are all tired beyond belief. I can feel you.

I can give you advice on ways to help you win. Please know that you are moving in a direction of safety and joy, despite the way in looks.

Your Health

Create a save haven for yourself. This means meditation, and body care through healthy food, massage and natural medicine. The Mother Earth, Gaia has wonderful healing herbs that help with the treatment of deliberate auto-immune diseases, now plaguing the planet. You can use new de-toxing modalities that can also help restore your health.

Remember that prevention is the best cure. In the times that you are living in there are many health threats. Know that the new deliberate auto-immune diseases cannot be treated effectively with prescription drugs or antibiotics. Avoid bug bites of all kinds. They are disease carriers. Perhaps you can bring nature inside with plants and fountains. Mosquito net tents for camping and being in the backyard during the summer months should be used.

An acid system is a big health problem, with many people, so do not drink soda pop because it makes the system acid! High stress people that stay addicted to soda, and coffee and toxic cigarettes are increasing the likelihood that they will get sick from colds or worse, from deadly auto-immune diseases.

The body needs all the help it can get in these times so be aware. Toxic emotions can make your system acid as well so remember to clear out negative emotions daily. Also, know that your liver and kidneys should be cleansed so they can fight off disease. Many things in your environment that can be harmful to your system so stay aware of these things. Be conscious in your eating and do not expose yourself to harmful chemicals. Drink lots of water for cleansing.

The parasitic nature of the anti-evolutionary forces is apparent in the ways their creations of economic monopolization, disease, poverty, and mind-control, affects the entire planet. Humans today want to heal this world and they are crying out from their hearts for relief.

The blinders that humans wear are getting so uncomfortable. Instigate radical change. 'Radical' is usually just the truth. Nevertheless, the truth has been distorted and manipulated for way too long. The People are exposing the intentions of the institutions of religion and government that hold power and control over the whole world. They are not going to relinquish power willingly, but when they are forced to, big changes will happen and these changes are in the accordance with God's will.

Remember what Anne Frank said, "all people are basically good." The problem has been the tendency for humans to blindly trust the enemy, because the enemy wears an accepted uniform. The Garments, Titles and Credentials of the material world often mask a deep black core. These evils of the anti-evolutionary forces are justified with arrogance. However, these Fronts are dissolving like the wicked witch made of sugar from the Wizard of Oz.

The Jewish people of the holocaust were sacrificial lambs, with soul contracts to demonstrate what can happen when a leader gets out of control. For Heaven's sake, please consider how certain strategies for power and control have been manifesting in your world politics.

Know that the apathy of your youth is partially due to mind-altering television and violent video games. While the youth tune out in these supposedly harmless forms of entertainment, what is the effect on their young minds?

These tactics work over time. The near extinction of the middle class and the decline of small businesses also plays into a deliberate strategy. Now without pointing fingers, I challenge you to discern how and who. The messages I give are a warning. So, protect yourself, your family and your community. Speak of these things to whoever will listen. Remember your mighty pen and your awesome communication technologies.

The population of your planet must learn to live in harmony with Nature and God. The stance on over population to certain manipulative leaders is to exterminate a large part of you. They seek to quickly and arrogantly solve the over population problem. Their agenda to be the 'best stock' (meaning themselves) left to carry on the human race is ruthless beyond sanity. The Legacy of Elitism and Arrogance at work, perhaps?

Sharing?
Oh Boy, I think we need to sit down for a minute. The changes will be graceful to a degree; we hope they will be, anyway.

Lady Magdalene:
Graceful change is my hope, as well. Nevertheless, *Planetary Birth* can be unpredictable. Go out in the world with much courage and love. Radiate Love and Light right out from your center and expand your power, to affect the whole scene. Meditate, if you like to meditate. Help change laws, if you would like a career in the political arena. That way you bring Light and Truth to the cause of protecting your American Constitution.

In this game of free-will there are no guarantees, so be willing to gamble on this battered planet's recovery from centuries of attack. Will someone hurt you, or crucify you in some way? Well maybe, so choose your own level of danger based on how well you think you can handle it.

God is our Mother with her healing treasures of the Earth,
God is our Father with his wondrous Worlds and Sciences,
Embrace our God as Mother and Father.
Dear Sisters,
Dear Brothers,
Fight not amongst yourselves.
Dear Lovers of a broken romantic dream,
Hold on, and fight the good fight to
Restore Love, Honor, Peace and Freedom to
the Whole Human Divine Family

Lady Magdalene

Straight Talk about Sex

Lady Magdalene:
"*Humankind has misunderstood the purpose of sex, and in searching for the returning to the Creator, has debased it. And because the founders of religion knew the truth of this returning, and did not wish the masses to attain it also, they forbade it, and thereby made it dominant. Part of the difficulty of male humankind moving from one woman to another in endlessness, stems from the misunderstanding and non-development of true exchange, and the purpose of this exchange.*"- *The Only Planet of Choice** Sex should be a spiritual union. It's that simple. The problems you have faced stem from the rewiring of humans. That was the work of the Forces of Darkness.

Sharing?
So the romantic dreams of women relate to this desire for a spiritual union with their husband?

Lady Magdalene:
Yes indeed. The relationship with the true husband, the woman's Twin Soul, is quite frankly, so completely fulfilling that there is no desire for any other man. This is by God's Design. Unfortunately with the '*rewiring*' that occurred, men were disconnected from their emotional bodies and became '*pollinators*' you might say, with no conception of why women have to be so 'emotionally clingy'. Then with the women disconnected from their center of power, the literal 'breeding ground' was set for centuries of unhappy women home with many children, as the men were out '*screwing around*'. Since men held all the power

and set all the rules, this became socially acceptable. The whole Ying/Yang imbalance was created by the Forces of Darkness. As humans are now becoming aware of this imbalance, they are also seeking their soulmates. However, the Ying/Yang energies of each individual must come back into balance, before the soulmate joining can manifest.

Sharing?
So with a sincere desire to balance the Ying/Yang energies within, the soulmate will appear in one's life?

Lady Magdalene:
This will eventually occur, yes. Although you may find, that he or she resides on the other side of the veil. This can be frustrating, but be not disheartened, because this signifies that you have evolved immensely! Happy graduation to you! May your blessed divine union, come full circle!

Sharing?
What advice can you give young women on how to survive in these times and keep their spirits in tack? Should they feel wrong about bringing a child into this world, because the world is on such shaky ground?

Lady Magdalene:
I would highly recommend that any young woman or man pursue spiritual development and learning of all kinds. I would also advise that they not grab onto the easiest thing to do for a living, out of laziness or boredom.

Judge not if a woman wants to have a baby. My hope is that every young woman wisely chooses for herself how she wants to make a living, or if she wants to start a family. The right to choose is her gift and his. It is also their way to not condemn this world, as to consider it unfit for new life! Let the younger generation unfold, you will be surprised at how progressive they are, as they easily embrace new thought.

Sharing?
No judgment, but sound advice for young adults. Thank you. We have seen how 'easy money' schemes can hurt people. The Hare could benefit from the ways of the patient Tortoise. I guess it's no accident that the symbol of the Mother Goddess is the turtle.

Lady Magdalene:
Yes indeed, the Mother Goddess is a supreme master of patience.

Sharing?
Can you comment on prostitution for us?

Lady Magdalene:
Do not get stuck in *getting rich quick schemes* that could hurt you. Yes girls, it is not casual to sell your body for money. I am speaking to young men also. The easy road to riches comes with a terrible price. The energy of those you have sex with will meld with yours. Do you want to degrade our own sacredness with acts of easy profit?

Do the men that chose to pay for what should be sacred; do they conceal the deed from their innocent, unsuspecting wives? Would you want to contribute to these women's pain?

The majority of humans on earth are not paired with their twin soul*. Will a trend toward men looking for a soulmate or their twin soul, ever become popular to men if they can continue to buy sex? Men often ignore the treasures of a spiritual. A sexual union that is spiritual as well, is much more fulfilling, is it not? Why not promote spiritual, sexual unions, dear ladies? These are important questions to ask yourself.

Besides the small amount of sexual healing therapists, that incorporate sex in a dignified and sacred way into their practice; how much of the energy of selling and buying sex, is dis-empowering? Is it worth the hurt that results from the emptiness of making a money deal out of something that should be a sacred sharing between soulmates or caring friends?

The Sacred Body Temple, seeks the fulfilling, enduring unconditional love and familiarity of the Twin Soul*. The road to this awesome form of love needs your patience and a commitment to develop over time, through loving sexual relationships. Be careful. The world of sexual desire, glamour and easy money seeks to allure the weak and the empty.

Sharing?
We appreciate knowing how you feel about sex and love. Can you comment on worshiping The Goddess?

Lady Magdalene:
Well I have been watching the spiritual trend of some that worship me as Isis. Some of the same hypocritical issues that I have seen with humans that worship Jesus, I have see with those that worship *The Goddess*. It is my hope that you may get it this time. Jesus and I do not want to be deified, nor does any of the other popular Ascended Masters. The teachings that Jesus and I represent must be lived from a pure heart.

Any Goddess worship that includes acts of abuse of power or ego gratification is missing the mark. When women get together and create their own hierarchy they are not supporting the ways of the Goddess. The jealous and the empty do not display *from their actions* the ways of Isis. The Christians blowing up abortion clinic do not display *from their actions* the ways of Jesus.

The Kingdom of God is within! Try not to fall into the old human traps of power, petty jealousy and ever hatred. Now what would Jesus want you to do? Do you hate men for what they did to you? Would the Goddess want you to hate?

Why not just follow the ways of these Master Beings. They want you to be love generators. What love have you put in your heart today? In a cold world of mundane survival, how much value is your warm smile, or kind deed? It is everything! It is being Jesus; it is being Isis, or Sister Aimee, or Mary Magdalene and that's what makes us smile. We want to see you living our teachings. We cry, seeing you stuck in a vicious cycle of hypocritical worship.

Are New Age People more spiritual than Christians because they are open to metaphysical truths? Not always. Some people are more developed in the heart, while others are more aware of truths that the Bible omits or distorts.

Sharing?
Point well taken. We have seen disgraceful acts of no love from both of these types of spiritual seekers.

'If you bring forth what is within you,
what you bring forth will save you,
If do not bring forth what is within you,
what you do not bring forth,
will destroy you"

Gospel of Thomas

Sister of Time

Bring it forth sister,
Bleed and cry and scream,
and when it is all purged,
Rise like Christ,
Because Resurrection & Eternal Life,
Belongs to Us All.

The Magdalene,
Sister of time,
Archetype of the divine female passion,
You rose from suffering,
and may your triumph be everyone's triumph,
over this dream-spell, There is no hell,
except in the mind,
Find Peace and Be Well.
Heaven's Dreams await you

Interconnected,
woven,
and bound to each other we are,
in this game of fate,
mixed with faith.
To gain Mastery,
that is why we are here we.
Ripe for a harvest and ready,
for an unraveling,
and re-creation, we are.
And like a Celtic lullaby
I wait in anticipation.
Because with God's severed connection to us, restored,
The Whole and Holy Human Grail Family,
will find their divinely ordered places,
in this Universe.

Lady Magdalene's Prayer
Dear Father/Mother, the Creator of us all, connect us to your heart, so we may feel safe and loved once again. In the illusions of The Matrix, we have become lost children. In a world gone mad we work to restore Goodness, Peace, Honor and Charity, and all the ways of The Light. Our world is healing and recovering and we gallantly love ourselves, deep in our Brave Hearts. May the miracles flow as our divine selves unfold before our very eyes. With the end of the reign of darkness and nightmares, let us manifest the future Heaven on Earth. We are blessed! The future good dreams of humankind live on.

Sharing?
We are a curious group and we have read many stories about your life that don't match what you have told us about yourself. We feel blessed that you shared with us your true-life story, thus exposing the lies that have been told for centuries. We would not want anyone to distort the truth any longer. Can we stop the disinformation surrounding your life?

Lady Magdalene:
Disinformation will teach you how to discern; that is an important lesson. I am giving you truth now. The shadow side within, that people mirror outwards, often influences what they choose to believe.

Some people will not be able to absorb the truth right away. Some books about me are partially true. Filter the information through your own heart. I challenge you to take the truth I have given you and when you go back and read that partial truth book, you will know what parts are real.

Disinformation is sort of like the 'Mirror Principle' at work. It is in the telling of stories that man shows his true colors, through the reflection in the mirror. I am a mirror, a powerful *archetype**, and how someone sees me, when they look at me, is always a reflection of themselves. This is not something to crusade against. I just gave you my story so if you wish, be so bold as to share this transmission with everyone. Believe me. The reactions will be diverse.

Know that certain *channeled books* about my life have truth and fiction mixed together. Furthermore, the nuances of the person doing the channeling will often come through. This is not something to judge, dear ones. If God didn't approve of this then *stone tablets from heaven* would be falling from the skies to educate you! Wouldn't that be ridiculous? Remember that a 100% perfect channeling is very rare and discernment is part of your education in this process.

Know that sometimes people channel beings from the *other side of the veil* that have intent to manipulate. A channeler may be pure of heart, but not always are the entities coming through them.

Sharing?
One book says that you and Jesus never had sex. However, this book does mention your relationship with the Roman Centurion. Can you comment on this book? The book also says that Martha was your sister.

Lady Magdalene:
The chapter called *The Waterfall* is beautiful truth, and I will cherish forever the time I spent with my Beloved at the waterfall of Baniass, Israel (Palestine). Some authors seemed to understand that *virgin conception* is a part of my story, however in my complete story I also had sex with Jesus, the normal way, so to speak, which is just as wonderful, just different.

Some books state that Martha was my sister. She was Mary of Bethany's sister, like the Bible says. However, I was Mary of Bethany and Mary of Magdala. This may surprise many. I thoroughly understand the confusion regarding this because the 3rd dimension has much limitation in comprehension. Limited understanding will change as human DNA reconnects back to 12 stands.

I truly appreciate the noble quest of recent authors and messengers telling stories about my life, however the time is ripe now, for total truth. May no stone be left unturned! This is the fiery side of myself speaking. Masters have personalities too. So you could say that even Ascended Masters will have different moods that come through, while being channeled by messengers. So understand that Ascended Masters have their humanness as well and this is not a bad thing. In this channeled book I must say that my fiery side is speaking, because the time for humanity to wake up is now!

The back-cover of this book claims to be exposing myths, lies and secrecy. Now for the bomb; the most important 'exposure' for you to learn about from this book has little to do with my personal autobiography. It has to do with opening your eyes to the truth regarding the agendas of The Bush Crime Family and the Illuminati; the creators of 9/11 and many, many other heinous acts that have transpired through the past 2000 years. Their time is up! God is ready to put them all on a very long time out, on a sphere to match their energy of greed, and power hungry lust. This act of God's Grace will allow '*the meek to inherit the Earth*'. The meek will become empowered! This will create a worldwide healing process that is long overdue.

Sharing?
That is very empowering to know! We love your radical side Lady Magdalene. We are also well aware of the radical attributes of your twin soul, Jesus. Many Christians do not like this radical nature and are appalled by those who speak of it.

Lady Magdalene:
They are afraid. The fear of the dark-side is deeply embedded within them. Courage could set them free and it is my hope that many will embrace '*the lion*' within! When *the lamb* and *the lion* unite within, true empowerment and free-dom can be won!

These mythic phrases I use relate to the *mirror principle*. Jesus and I are the archetypes that hold many meanings for different types of people. How many different stories about Jesus' life has man written in different books? Thousands perhaps?

Sharing?
The number of books about Jesus is probably more than a hundred thousand. The '*Mirror Principle*' and diverse reactions that you speak of, is well demon-strated by the movie, 'The Last Temptation of Christ'. When it was first released in 1988, protesters firebombed movie theaters, slashed movie screens and fights broke out in the streets. This movie was controversial, but why the violence? The scene that showed Jesus in a romantic relationship with you must have caused the violent reaction. However, portraying you as a prostitute that Jesus was seeing *romantically* was a bit much to believe. Obviously some people take every thing about Jesus very seriously. Maybe they believe that the virgin Jesus should never have a lover on Earth because of his purity, and that God must have him paired with a lily-white angel!

Lady Magdalene:
Well there are many types of angels. Some choose to get right down on the planet with you to get an experience of what it is like to be a human on Earth.

I have received quite an invaluable education through many incarnations. I am in service to humanity. All of those in service to humanity and living many incarnations on Earth are incarnated angels of some kind.

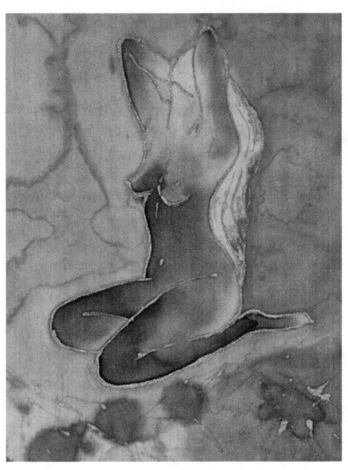

Sexual Joy
is not a sin, imagine that.

Answer to the riddle:
The Sacrament of The Last Supper
by Salvador Dali

☽☽   ✡   **15**   ✡   ☽☽

The Ascension Then & Now

A Graduation into Eternal Life

Sharing?
Will you share with us your experience of the Crucifixion and Resurrection of
Jesus?

Lady Magdalene:
Yes I will; although I cannot go into the traumatic and painful aspects of it,
because you have already been bludgeoned with those stories that have been
told repeatedly.

The Act of Atonement*, or the Crucifixion/Resurrection was a planned act
of Atonement that was directed by the Spiritual Hierarchy, through God's
sanction.

The need for the Act of Atonement came about because the Jewish people
failed to accept their own Messiah's teachings. This probability was foreseen
hundreds of years before Christ was ever born.

The ability to resurrect a life is real. The ancient Egyptians studied the ways of
resurrection and ascension, to reach immortality. It is a spiritual science.

So the most idealistic hope was that Christ would have been highly successful
in shifting the consciousness of The Hebrews, to avoid the Act of Atonement

(the crucifixion). If their consciousness would have shifted, then he could have demonstrated his ascension, without a crucifixion needing to take place.

Sharing?
So what you are saying is that the Hebrews failed the test?

Lady Magdalene:
That is a negative why of looking at it. Let us just say that they were not ready, and so the window for shifting to Christ Consciousness closed. However, now it is open again, and this current window is going to close at the end of 2012.

Sharing?
Now it is for everyone to shift into Christ Consciousness?

Lady Magdalene:
Yes, everyone, every race, every human and every living thing. It is a level of development, the level that we as a *planet* are on now.

Sharing?
You mentioned earlier that the Roman Centurion pierced Jesus' side in a strategic spot while he was on the cross to convince the other Roman soldiers that Jesus was dead, and that breaking his legs would not be necessary. Can you comment on that?

Lady Magdalene:
Yes, this was true, and then the Roman Centurion reduced Christ suffering by placing a cloth soaked in belladonna mixed with gall (an alcohol) up to his face. His body was removed from the cross within a short time after this. His blessed Resurrection from death was certainly a holy miracle. However, miracles can be common occurrences for anyone and should never be regarded as rare occurrences for only perfectly divine beings. Did you know that Peter really did walk on water? It was only after a fear thought entered his mind, that he reached for Jesus' hand, because he started to sink into the water.

It is important to know that Jesus developed his spirit through many past lives and for thousands of years. He never claimed that anything he did, could not be done by another spiritual aspirant. And every human living today has lived many lives so all of humanity is ready for this. It is the next step for all humans on earth now.

The truth is that the Ascension is for every human being, however, not through a crucifixion/resurrection type experience. The Planetary Ascension experience for humans today, involves diligent dedication to focusing on one's spiritual growth. There are two things that are most important to focus on right now. They are emotional body healing and balancing the ying and yang energies within.

If you wish, you can develop an understanding of how Ascension works. I would recommend you read 'The Ancient Secret of the Flower of Life', by Drunvalo Melchizedek.* But this is truly extra credit. The major requirement is the emotional body healing and awakening to truth (and the truth you will not find on TV news or from Christian fundamentalism).

I have an extra credit lesson in *metaphysics* and *sacred geometry* to give you. I will refer to Salvador Dali's rendition of The Last Supper to help me relay the concept of Ascension to you. Look at the painting titled '*The Sacrament of the Last Supper*', by Salvador Dali.

To view the painting go to www.ellensplace.net/dali.html

Lady Magdalene interprets the painting by Salvador Dali, 'The Sacrament of The Last Supper'

Now, if you examine the middle, top portion of the painting you will see Christ's *Ascended Light Body**. In the painting the shape of the window is very important and it represents the *Mer-Ka-Ba** Ascension Light-Ship of Sacred Geometry. The famous artist Salvador Dali is telling you, that Jesus was telling you, (by pointing up with his finger) about the process of Ascension*. The significance of The Apostles shown with their heads down on the table is obviously characteristic of their shame, fear, denial and unreadiness to absorb the concept.

Now I am going to quote the artist. This is what Dali said about his painting, 'The Sacrament of The Last Supper':

This painting represents an "arithmetic and philosophical cosmogony based on the paranoiac* sublimity* of the number twelve … the pentagon contains microcosmic man: Christ"*

So what was Dali saying here, can you read between the lines?

Sharing?
We are trying.

Lady Magdalene:
It's a brain twister so let me break it down for you. If any one of you has attended a 'Flower of Life Workshop', you would be on top of the mystery.

'An arithmetic and philosophical cosmogony':
Dali is pointing out that the physics of stellar phenomena in relation to the evolution of the universe, is profoundly important and it relates to *Sacred Geometry** which is arithmetic (referring to the mathematics of evolution). The shape of the Mer-Ka-Ba Ascension Ship* is pentagonal. This is the shape of the window in *'The Sacrament of the Last Supper'* painting by Dali. Christ's Light Body is sort of floating in the middle upper portion of the painting.

'based on the paranoiac sublimity of the number twelve':
Perhaps Dali is saying that some view the number twelve as so profound, (a hint of apostolic succession arrogance) but the real magnum-opus, is the awe-inspiring pentagonal symbol (the dodecahedron) which relates to man's Mer-Ka-Ba Ascension Ship*
The Mer-Ka-Ba is the energy spaceship for the spirit, and Christ experienced entering his Mer-Ka-Ba Ascension Light-Ship*

'the pentagon contains microcosmic man: Christ':
Dali is saying that we should honor the sublime* nature of the pentago-nal Mer-Ka-Ba*, which far exceeds in sublimity of a linear twelve, (Apostolic Succession). In other words Dali is showing us that Christ was teaching us to honor the 'circle way', not the patriarchal hierarchy way! Leonardo DaVinci understood all of this. He understood about the male/female balance within, that is a requirement to reaching the Ascension. The Apostles, not understand-ing this, because they were born into a patriarchal society; had an inborn disad-vantage to understanding Christ's Ascension process. I was developed in both my male and female energies enough to understand that the wounds of patri-archy would be carried into the future, through their misunderstanding. That was quite heartbreaking for me. I was a seer and I could see a future of war and imbalance that would carry the wounds of patriarchy far into the future. I was traumatized in the weeks to come after Christ resurrection.

The dodecahedron is any polyhedron (a solid figure having many plane faces). The dodecahedron has twelve (five sided) plane faces. A pentagon is a five sided polygon. The sacredness of the dodecahedron relates to its significance as part of the Mer-Ka-Ba, the Ascension Light Ship for the human body. The Mer-Ka-Ba contains Christ, and Christ is the Microcosmic man (the *model* of the divine yet human man, meaning all humans). This sacred geometry as it relates to the ascension, is for all humans to grasp and experience, and Christ and I knew this. The seeds for this learning were planted through Christ's Ascension. Now is harvest time, and Christ wants you to understand that it is your turn to ascend into a higher dimension!

The shroud was real. The impression that was burned into the cloth was caused from the spirit of Christ Michael leaving Jesus' physical body. And then Jesus came back into full human consciousness.

The etheric energy cord was not severed, which makes it possible to come back from physical death. Christ was tethered to Earth, by myself and Mother Mary; we were the guardians of Christ's etheric cord, in the time between the Crucifixion and the Resurrection.

Sharing?
In our research, we have found your 1983 channeling, through Elizabeth Clare Prophet. Is this message from you? We will quote a part of it.

"The Omega Light, that He might soar as the Fire of God's own Love and that His Flame might leap into the hearts of the whole world and abide there forever and forever until that Fire should melt and dissolve and consume and transmute all resistance to its Eternal Flame."

Lady Magdalene:
Yes, those were my words and the point is to surrender to God, as Christ did for us all. To stubbornly resist (product of the ego) surrendering to God's will, will not serve you. You resist growth and change. Why resist the exciting journey to God, and the enjoyment of the gifts of God? Why fear becoming aware that you are God and you can create anything you want from nothing (the void*)

His Flame (His Passionate Intention) would enter the Consciousness of Man and melt, dissolve, consume and transmute Man's resistance, to becoming more. His Ascension planted the seed into the *Consciousness of Man* to know that one day you will all experience Ascension as well.

Christ's physical body was removed from the cross and carried to the property of Joseph of Arimathea. For a period of three days, He was held in The Void*.

After the three days had passed, I saw him in his higher dimension state, (in his Light Body; see Book of Mary, Chapter 5, passage 8 & 9). "Lord, I saw you today in a vision. He answered and said to me,
'Blessed are you that you did not waver at the sight of Me.'

This vision that I saw was real, but at the time I did not know it was really an angel showing me that Christ had risen.
The angel approached me as I was in a state of deep prayer for his return. He said 'I have not yet ascended to my Father'. I saw him, smiled and I reached for him. However it was not Jesus, and the angel that showed me 'His Ascended state' said, do not touch me.

Christ had risen from his 3rd dimensional body into his healed Light Body. The Shroud of Turin is proper evidence of the metamorphosis that occurred. As I learned of his resurrection, I was elevated and ecstatic! My Love was quickly ready, for me to go out and tell the Apostles that he had Risen! Telling the others that he had Risen, was an absolute joy!

Christ's Light Body went out to visit several of his followers, so many people saw him in his Light Body; which was lowered enough in vibration to be seen.

Now, to give more references regarding the pentagon, realize that the feared five-pointed star, the pentagram is on the floor of The *Tower of Magdala*, built by Sauniere. As humans we fear what we do not understand. It was those who wished to breed fear and to control others, that created the myth, that what was sublime was evil. The pentagram is not evil.

Dali was saying that Christ was the Microcosmic Man*, but this is also true for every human. We all have the same *Divine Birthright* to Ascend into Eternal Life, like Jesus did and stop the need for traveling around the Karmic (astrological) Wheel. We can graduate and rise above the necessity to reincarnate repeatedly. Reincarnation was never intended to be endless.

Within the Macrocosm (the universe itself), contains The Microcosm (a system more or less analogous to a much larger system in constitution, configuration or development.). Man is the microcosmic representation of God. We are God, in that sense. I hope that this might clear up some of the misunderstanding regarding the phrase 'Jesus is God' *exclusively*. You are God also, my dear friends.

It is all within and you have to get in to get out! This is the mystery of the Holy Grail. The 'Holy Bloodline' of Christ includes every human because we are all God's children. The Mary of Bethany bloodline, the Jesus & Mary Magdalene bloodline and every bloodline on the planet, are special and divine! Jesus' level of divinity is the *Divine Birthright* of every human. We all carry the potential to reach full Christ Consciousness through our devotion to spiritual growth.

'The Ancient Secret of The Flower of Life' (volume one) & (volume two) by Drunvalo Melchizedek*, are great books that share metaphysical information related to Ascension and the Mer-Ka-Ba.

The Holon of Balance Octahedron

An easy tool to bring peace and balance
to situations and people experiencing
volatile emotions in these times

Lady Magdalene:
I would like to introduce to you the Holon of Balance. This visualization tool was designed to be simple for people to use during these last days of intense energy. Every day the increase of energy will be causing a huge intensification of what is already going on with people. Those people that are fighting battles inside themselves will be further traumatized as each incoming '*extreme wave activity*' coming from deep space, increases all of the thoughts and feelings that are coming from within them. Visualize two, four-sided pyramids, one is pointing up and the other pointing down, and they touch at the bases. Visualize the person (yourself or another) inside the middle of the Holon of Balance. Doing this will stabilize their energy and keep them in balance. For more details on this powerful yet simple visualization tool go online to www.tomkenyon.com/hathors.php

Sharing:
Do we have to breathe a certain way like in certain meditations?

Lady Magdalene:
No and its simplicity is a blessing because when you are traumatized you may be having a hard time focusing. This simple visualization is very powerful! Peace be with you.

Lady Magdalene:
The time is now for the *Second Coming of Christ* in all of you! From the seeds that were planted by Christ 2000 years ago, humanity is now ready to blossom. This 2000 year planetary germination period has taught humanity all about the horrors of war, hatred and jealousy. Now if there is still war, hatred and jealousy in your own heart it will not work. So, please be of *Good Courage* and be not discouraged, as to the state of the world. We are all microcosms of the macrocosm! In our changing as individuals, the whole world changes! Remember to be the change that you wish to see in the world.

Also know that every individual will have his or her own timing and way. Transformation comes in many shapes and sizes. Remember that everyone must go within and find peace within his or her own heart and mind. People must begin the Ascension process by clearing their own emotional body first. Learning the *Mer-Ka-Ba meditation* is not necessary; it is just something to learn about, if you choose.

When the actual ascension of the entire planet happens, it will be comparable to birth. Now every mother knows that whether they took Lamaze classes or not, that baby is going to be born. Mothers know that the birth process goes smoother when she does not move into fear. It is like that. Therefore, the best preparation is just simple prayer, meditation and emotional body clearing. For now just go within and heal your heart wounds and do not worry.

You are now co-creating this planet's future. You have proven with your good works, that you can alter the path of destruction that was predicted in The Book of Revelations. By your own doing, you altered the course for the betterment of all of mankind. God and the ascended ones helped you, but you did it! You stayed connected and people prayed. You held so much Light that you almost reached critical mass, one time already. That is incredible!

Now, does this seem too good to be true, that God really has an intelligent plan for your salvation and Ascension into Eternal Life? If you think not, I must say, oh dear child of little faith, you need to remember the wonderment of being a child of Heaven!

The Book of Mary

Sharing?
What happened to the Gospel According to Mary Magdalene, called the Book of Mary*? Did you give it to Joseph of Arimathea along with the Holy Grail?

Lady Magdalene:
No, I did not give it to Joseph of Arimathea, I gave it to Jesus shortly after I wrote it. He gave it to the Roman Centurion and he was told where to hide it, for safekeeping. The Roman Centurion took it to the Great Pyramids of Egypt. He attempted to enter the Hall of Records through its entranceway, which is at the right paw of the Sphinx. However, he was attacked from behind and it was stolen from him.

Sharing?
The right paw of the Sphinx had a hidden chamber for storing secret knowledge?

Lady Magdalene:
Yes, and the Ancient Atlantian documents were held there as well. Isis and Osiris (citizens from Atlantis) used the vault.

In 1945 in Nag Hammadi, Egypt, earthenware jars, filled with 46 scriptures was found. The treasures of these 'biographies of Christ' included, The Book of Mary.

The Gospel According to Mary Magdalene,
*also called **'The Book of Mary'***

Starts with Chapter 4 (*Pages 1 to 6 of the manuscript, containing chapters 1-3 are lost. The extant text starts on page 7.*)
One story states that a woman burned some of the scrolls in the fireplace for kindling, before she learned of their significance. Perhaps that is why pages are missing or perhaps there was another reason why the pages are missing?

Magdalene's comments in bold type

..... Will matter then be destroyed or not?**(in reference to Revelations)**
22) The Savior said, all nature, all formations,
     all creatures exist in and with

one another, and they will be
resolved again into their own roots
(Planetary Ascension coming in our lifetime)

23) For the nature of matter is resolved
into the roots of its own nature alone.
(We will go to our divinely ordered places)

24) He who has ears to hear, let him hear.

25) Peter said to him,
Since you have explained everything to us, tell
us this also: What is the sin of the world?

26) The Savior said There is no sin,
but it is you who make sin
when you do the things that are like the nature of adultery,
which is called sin.
(Sin exists in the illusion of duality)

27) That is why the Good came into your midst,
to the essence of every nature in order to
restore it to its root.

28) Then He continued and said,
That is why you become sick and die,
for you are deprived of the one who can heal you.

29) He who has a mind to understand,
let him understand.

30) Matter gave birth to a passion that has no equal,
which proceeded from something contrary
to nature. Then there arises a disturbance
in its whole body.

31) That is why I say to you, Be of good courage,
and if you are discouraged be encouraged
in the presence of the different forms of nature.

32) He who has ears to hear, let him hear.

33) When the Blessed One had said this,
He greeted them all, saying,
Peace be with you. Receive my peace unto yourselves.

34) Beware that no one lead you astray saying
Lo here or lo there!
For the Son of Man is within you.**(Follow your heart)**

35) Follow after Him!

36) Those who seek Him will find Him.

37) Go then and preach the gospel of the Kingdom.
38) Do not lay down any rules
beyond what I appointed you, and do not give a law
like the lawgiver lest you be constrained by it.
39) When He said this he departed.

Chapter 5

But they were grieved.
They wept greatly, saying,
how shall we go to the Gentiles
and preach the gospel of the Kingdom of the Son of Man
If they did not spare Him, how will they spare us?

Then Mary stood up, greeted them all, and said to her brethren, Do not weep and do not grieve nor be irresolute, for His grace will be entirely with you and will protect you. **(Faith wisdom)**
But rather, let us praise His greatness, for He has prepared us and made us into Men. **(I understood that Jesus regarding me as equal to the men)**
When Mary said this, she turned their hearts to the Good,
and they began to discuss the words of the Savior.

1) Peter said to Mary, Sister we know that the Savior loved you more than the rest of woman.
Tell us the words of the Savior which you remember which you know, but we do not,
nor have we heard them.
2) Mary answered and said,
What is hidden from you I will proclaim to you.
3) And she began to speak to them these words: I, she said, I saw the Lord in a vision and I said to Him,
Lord I saw you today in a vision.
He answered and said to me,
4) Blessed are you that you did not waver at the sight of Me.
For where the mind is there is a treasure.
5) I said to Him, Lord how does he who sees the vision see it,
6) through the soul or through the spirit?
7) The Savior answered and said,
He does not see through the spirit,

8)   but the mind that is between the two
      that is what sees the vision and it is.....
      (The third eye* sees the vision)

(pages 11-14 are missing from the manuscript.)

Chapter 8

.....it.
10)   And desire said, I did not see you descending,
       but now I see you ascending.
       Why do you lie since you belong to me?
11)   The soul answered and said, I saw you.
       You did not see me nor recognize me.
       I served you as a garment and you did not know me.
       When it said this,
       it (the soul) went away rejoicing greatly.
12)   Again it came to the third power,
       which is called ignorance.
13)   The power questioned the soul, saying,
       Where are you going?
       In wickedness are you bound.
       But you are bound; do not judge!
14)   And the soul said, Why do you judge me,
       although I have not judged?
15)   I was bound, though I have not bound.
16)   I was not recognized.
       But I have recognized that the All is being dissolved,
       both the earthly things and the heavenly.
17)   When the soul had overcome the third power,
       it went upwards
       and saw the fourth power,
       which took seven forms. *(See Seven Veils*)*
18)   The first form is darkness, the second desire,
       the third ignorance, the fourth is the excitement of death,
       the fifth is the kingdom of the flesh,
       the sixth is the foolish wisdom of flesh,
       the seventh is the wrathful wisdom.
       These are the seven powers of wrath.

(See the Seven Veils* in the glossary of terms)

19) They asked the soul,
    Whence do you come slayer of men,
    or where are you going, conqueror of space?
20) The soul answered and said,
    What binds me has been slain,
    and what turns me about has been overcome.
21) And my desire has been ended and ignorance has died.
22) In an aeon*, I was released from a world,
    and in a type from a type,
    and from the fetter of oblivion which is transient.
23) From this time on will I attain to the rest of the time,
    of the season, of the aeon*, in silence.

Chapter 9

1) When Mary had said this, she fell silent,
   since it was to this point that the Savior
   had spoken with her.
2) But Andrew answered and said to the brethren,
   Say what you wish to say about what she has said.
   I at least do not believe that the Savior said this.
   For certainly these teachings are strange ideas.
3) Peter answered and spoke concerning these same things.
4) He questioned them about the Savior:
   Did He really speak privately with a woman and not openly with us?
   Are we to turn about and all listen to her?
   Did he prefer her to us?
5) Then Mary wept and said to Peter, My brother Peter,
   what do you think?
   Do you think that I have thought this up myself in my heart,
   or that I am lying about the Savior?
6) Levi answered and said to Peter,
   Peter you have always been hot tempered.
7) Now I see you contending against the woman like the adversaries.
8) But if the Savior made her worthy,
   who are you indeed to reject her?
   Surely the Savior knows her very well.
9) That is why He loved her more than us.

Rather let us be ashamed and put on the perfect Man,
and separate as He commanded us and preach the gospel,
not laying down any other rule or other law
beyond what the Savior said.
10) And when they heard this
they began to go forth to proclaim and to preach.
http://www.gnosis.org/library/marygosp.htm

Magdalene Speaks to Peter

My dear little brother,
archetype of the old Piscean Age,
surely now you can see,
that the 'strange ideas' I had not made up,
in my own head,
and yet without my heart, fully connected,
and grounded in love for thy Father/Mother,
both aspects of thy Creator,
without that connection, I surely would be
lost, without the eyes to see, or the ears to hear,
and while The Great Mystery, of our divinity
unfolds day by day,
I still stand alone and lonely in my heart,
2000 years later,
waiting to share the bliss with all my brothers and sisters,
that are still not awake to The Bliss of The Great Mystery,
and yet in my dreams you are all there,
as we dine once again at His Table,
The Eternal Supper, the eternal nourishment,
of our realized Godliness, co-creators, dreaming,
and creating into the future.
The Eternal Supper,
I hope you to see you there,
My Dear Brother Peter.

🕯🕯 ✡ **16** ✡ 🕯🕯

Reunion of Twin Souls

Lady Magdalene:
Dear ladies and gentlemen if you are listening, have you ever wondered why people dream up certain phrases, terms of endearment and romantic poetry?

Sharing:
It is about our broken romantic dreams, unfulfilled and squelched in the age of patriarchy. On this planet poetry is mostly written by the wounded hearts.

Lady Magdalene:
Yes, but some of these visionaries saw far beyond the wounds of love. The longing can hurt and like the missing piece that would complete you, your emptiness awaits fulfillment. I wrote a poem to share that feeling of longing for The Beloved. Here it is.

Loving My Beloved

Like candy for a little girl,
you are yummy,

like the sunset for Mother Gaia
you are nurturing,

like The Father's engulfing embrace
you are protective,

like rain for my thirsty soul
you are the Water-Bearer
and my Garden is Resurrected,
.................and I want you..........

and I miss you...

and I miss you...

and I miss you...

... like the desserts miss the rain,
... like the desserts miss the rain,
... like the desserts miss the rain,

and I long for you...

and I long for you...

and I long for you...

... I belong no where else,
    ... I belong no where else,
        ... I belong no where else,

I belong in your arms...
    I belong in your arms...
        I belong in your arms...

.....Lady Magdalene to Prince Esu Immanuel

Lady Magdalene:
So, you may be wondering why I am not in his arms now? Well, I am and parts of me are not. Image the soul as multi-dimensional and in many places.
Have you ever imagined being in more than one body, so you could get more things accomplished? Well, this is what Ascended Masters sometimes do to serve God and humanity. This level of service relates to the energy of 777.

The energy of twin flames (twin souls) united in serving God and humanity is the energy of 777, and the portal of the Mystical Marriage. You may be an individual who eats, sleeps, walks, talks and breathes The Light. You may feel like such an odd anomaly and your friends wonder why you sit home alone on a Friday night with no date, because as far as they can tell, you think that no one is good enough for you. Perhaps you have *forced a fit*, many times before and you just know in your heart that your prince is *out there* somewhere? But where, you cry! Perhaps through your soul's agreement your partner did not incarnate on the planet with you? If this is the case for you, then get excited, because the Ascension will bring you together with him or her and I don't mean just through meditation!

Sharing?
Ok. We are very much looking forward to this! (blushing)

Lady Magdalene:
I feel your excitement. Divine sexual joy with your twin soul ... my.... my! Sex has become such a taboo subject in your world because of the debasement of it through 'The Battle of The Sexes'.

The Goddess Priestesses of Avalon prepared me to understand the Divine Union that was coming in my future. They were the ones who knew who I was on a soul level, the ones who showed me what womanhood was all about. They were my surrogate mothers that went far beyond what my birth mother was able to teach me.

By the time I met Jesus in Avalon I was a trained High Priestess of the Goddess. The Priest and The Priestess ... wow.... now that was romantic. He was blushing when he told me that Joseph (of Arimathea) sent him to see me because I was destined to become his new friend. That was the first thing he said to me and then we went for a walk. We were both a little shy at first, but we bonded quickly; for the overwhelming feeling of familiarity that we both felt was invoking our passion.

Sharing?
We read this beautiful passage about you and Jesus receiving gifts, can you comment?
From the book 'I Remember Union'*, by Flo Calhaun, about our gifts from Spirit:
"My gift was a headdress of crystal starlight, woven into the strands of my hair, overlaying my third eye in the center of my forehead, giving me continued vision, bathed in rainbows of light. They called it Hope, as they placed it gently on my head. The gift they gave to Jesus was a matrix of pure gold, a scepter which they placed within his heart, the symbol of Christ. They called it Love."

Lady Magdalene:
Sharing this with you is a blessing I have waited for, for a long wearisome time. I hope the author feels my thanks for relaying those exquisite words that describe one of my most cherished memories of all time.

Sharing?
That is so beautiful! Does our Ascending mean that we will meet our twin soul (Twin Flame)?

Lady Magdalene:
Most likely, yes. And this may be a meeting in meditation, because for right now, he or she is most likely on the other side of the veil. The thinning veil.... oh yes.... your magic day could be just around the corner. As you are healing and growing the veils are lifting one at a time. The *777 portal of the Mystical Marriage**.... oh yes.... that is your coming gift from God.... and it exquisitely beautiful!

Be ready in your heart. Heal, erase, delete, and transmute any old feelings or illusions of abandonment or betrayal. Then you will not be blocked from receiving him or her. This can be healing wounds caused from the age patriarchy, for some. *'The Battle of The Sexes'* program from The Lucifer Mind*; you will need to delete that. After you are cleared, you will be ready t o receive.

And so it will be that the Earth and all her inhabitants will return to their divinely ordered places. Earth's Birth into the next dimension of consciousness will bring many Twin Souls and Soul Groups together. In the New Golden Age, Twin Soul Love will light the way to the natural fulfillment and joy that is your Divine Birthright to receive.

Sara in Meditation

Lady Magdalene's quiet messages submerged into Sara's thoughts, usually between 4 and 6 am, before her children were awake. This is one of the messages, that is outside of the question and answer, channeling sessions.

Sara feels so lonely for a mate that would totally fulfill her. Since her divorce five years ago, she had stayed away from men altogether, to honor herself and to heal. She asks Lady Magdalene if there is a perfect mate for her?

Lady Magdalene shows Sara the symbol of the *Vesica Piscis** to go along with her message to Sara.

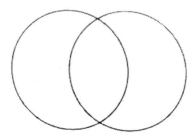

Lady Magdalene:
"Be not sad, dear Sara, he is coming into your life soon."

Sara met her twin soul a month later. They are now married and they have retreated to their private paradise home; out of the limelight, as they prefer to be.

The two circles of the *Vesica Piscis*, are symbolic of the magic of twin soul union. When you are whole within, you can merge with your twin flame's energy, to explore the sacredness of ascending to Heaven with the other half of oneself. The truth is that at this point you are not really a half; you are a whole submerging with your other whole. This concept is shown through the symbol of the two circles submerging into one.

The twin souls can one day return home to The Father and then back down to The Mother, to live safely in her womb. That returning happens when the two circles or two whole individuals submerge back into their oneness. Twin soul merging is so joyful and high and it's beyond words to describe. It is truly a gift from God.

Magdalene reveals her most private thoughts

This conversation between Jesus and Mary, Lady Magdalene shared with Sara in the middle of a quiet night. The conversation occurred right after she was almost stoned to death by her people.

Jesus

'My darling', (she is crying uncontrollably) I love you now, I love you forever and we will reside in Heaven's Realm, together forever, I promise you that. But today is hard and tomorrow may bring more ... he stops himself.

Mary:

Just touch me my Love, I do not want to see it now, ok. I will break, don't you see?

Jesus:

I know my darling. I am so sorry, my Mary.

Mary:

I am a mortal woman, my Rabboni. I am not as strong as you think I am.

Jesus:

Just relax my Mary, its ok. Peace be in your heart, my love. Do not worry, tonight I will stay with you, and I will keep my arms around you. He started to sing to her. Mother Mary comes in the room. Mother Mary joined in with the singing. They healed her bruised body as they sung to her in healing tones. She fell asleep.

Christ lay down with her and when they awoke the next morning, he told her to pack for a trip. They went to the Masada Mountain fortress caves, the home of the Essenes. Upon arrival *The Council* was ready to convene. With sadness, Christ spoke of the shift in plans that Mother Mary and The Spiritual Hierarchy had expected would come about. The visions of Christ's crucifixion and resurrection were coming on strong by the 'seers' of The Christ Group*.

Jesus and The Christ Group* discussed the ways in which His teachings would be carried into the future. Who would be *the Leader of His Movement* after the Resurrection? Who would that be? His thoughts focused on honoring His Magdalene for all that she was. He truly loved her passionately and deeply. She comprehended His teachings and integrated them within her heart with utmost humbleness.

He saw into the future and he felt his aching heart as they physically parted. He was torn between His human desire to marry her and His duty to The Mission to carry His ministry into the future with a qualified leader, after His Ascension back to The Father. He felt that Magdalene was the only one who qualified. *The Council* expressed the concern that appointing me as the *Leader of the Movement* would surely not work, because they knew that His male apostles had not risen to the level of consciousness that would accept a woman to lead them. The meeting with *The Council* closed with no final decision being made.

Knowing that he would be crucified was very painful for her. Her heart just about broke. She cried for days after he told her of their fate. Their love was put to the test, the test of self-sacrifice for the good of all. They were both Redeemers for humanity, which required their huge personal sacrifice. They had to transform their love into strong courage, because without them, humanity was in grave danger. The act of Atonement* through the plan of the *Crucifixion and Resurrection*, was the only hope.

An emotional adjustment period followed, after Christ gave Magdalene the news of their fate. Mary Magdalene tried so hard to not fall into the lower human feelings of betrayal that she felt about the Jewish people, her own people that crucified her with rocks. The human side of her felt the failure of the Jewish people, not choosing to fully embrace Christ's teachings, as a personal jab in her bleeding heart. She did not know how she could cope and go on knowing that she would lose her Rabonni. She pushed it out of her mind, as Jesus swept her away to go on a healing vacation.

They hiked to a waterfall of Baniass Israel (Palestine). In the waterfall the sacred waters sent the two of them out of their bodies to take flight into the Heavens. They joined with The Father in their hearts and minds.

The experience was beneficial as 'practice' for the crucifixion/resurrection drama, that would soon play out, besides being extremely healing to their souls. He said to her, "we can do anything my love, worry not, it will be ok."

They arrived back from Baniass with a renewed resolve. *The Last Supper* was planned with *The Council*. With their emotions high the two lovers courageously faced the next stage of their destinies. The emotions of Christ on their last days together, are clearly expressed in the music of the legendary Led Zeppelin. The song called '*In the Light*', clearly showed that Robert Plant was a channel, for Christ's emotions, through his evocative music.

Meet the Seven Christ Children of Today!

Faith
If ye have the faith of a grain of mustard seed, than watch what happens now, as the whole world Ascends into the next dimension of consciousness!

Magdalene's recipe for Faith Healing
2 cups of passionate Love for Our Heavenly Father
2 cups of respect and Love for The Divine Mother
2 cups of surrender to Divine Love & Light
(this prepares the Heart and Mind to receive)
4 cups of Brotherly & Sisterly Love
add this to Joy & Co-Create
with Love, Peace & Truth
Bake in the warm oven of your consciousness & heart.

Joseph of Abundance,
The future metaphoric leader of The Indigo Children, Crystal Children and their children's children. Mary Magdalene and Jesus had a son they named Joseph. He is in a sense 'born again' through the Holy Genetics of the New 12 Strand DNA, of the New Children being born today!

Harmony,
The sound healing from Venus, ushering in The New Age of Peace. Shalom, the Hebrew word for peace, holds the vision for The Hebrews to recognize their Divine Home, the Planet Venus.

Joy,
The best healer of all, is Joy! Divine Bliss is Your Birthright!

Charity,
Charity is all about giving to those that are in need. Cast thy bread upon the waters and see in return back, sevenfold. This is Universal Law.

Mercy,
God's Great Mercy in these end times. The distress in the next few years my cause some crazy things to happen to people, out of their fear and confusion. Know that all is forgiven with great compassion.

Grace,
The coming transition into the next dimension of consciousness, The Planetary Ascension, is expected to happen very gracefully. This great grace has been created by all the people that have prayed for it. Prayer works miracles!

Soul Families & Twin Souls Reunite

The universe operates in an orderly fashion. We are here in this experience and this life to ascend upward and experience joy. The immortal soul is striving to return to Source*. The long descent is over and we are now on the upward swing of the spiral dance, circling to reunite with our soul family and twin soul. This magical, wonderful, blissful gift, at the end of our long journey, adds the needed fulfillment that we have felt was missing all along, because it was.

Your earthly family is very different from your soul family. When you meet a soul family member, you may get a sense of feeling that you have known the person your whole life. This person from ages past has most definitely traveled through time with you and a true spiritual bond is eminent. Sometimes we will have soul family members in our earthly family. Think of your own biological family; which members do you feel closer to? There could be a good reason for this.

*"The familiarity with our soul family developed during the gestation period of creation, with the division of groups from the One. Though we speak of our group soul, ultimately there is no separate group to which we belong. We belong to all, for we were once a part of every group in the descent from the Source. Yet each group existed as a separate entity for an incalculable time on the descent into form. In its wholeness each group possessed a distinct character, and that character permeated the embryonic souls within it. The uniqueness of the group is forever reflected in those individuals whose formative prebirth occurred in its embrace."** This best describes sacred geometry in regards to souls. In this division process, the last division is the split of a twin soul, and this last split divides the feminine aspect of the twin, from the masculine aspect of the twin.

In the case of the Twin Soul couple, Mary Magdalene and Jesus, we can witness the trials and the beauty of a twin soul relationship lived in service and devotion to humanity and to our Creator. They certainly were married from the moment they laid eyes on each other. Their bond of love lives in timelessness, in the Holy Land of God's Womb.

The healing teams of twin souls are forming to create Heaven on Earth. This joy and spiritual bliss is the divine birthright of every human. Rejoice! The gift of twin soul reunion is attainable for every human!

A Quote from the late Bulgarian master,
Omraam Mikhael Aivanhov

"Every human being has a twin soul. When man leapt like a spark from the bosom of his Creator he was two in one, and these two parts complemented each other perfectly, each was the other's twin. These two halves became separated, they took different directions, and they have evolved separately. If they come to recognize each other at any point during their evolution, it is because each carries the image of the other in the depth of his being, each has put his seal on the other. Thus, each carries the image of this twin soul within. The image may be blurred but it is there. For this reason, everyone who comes on earth has a vague hope that he will meet somewhere a soul who will be everything he needs, and that with this soul he will find indescribable harmony and perfect fusion."*

A Book to Share

"The earthly family is a preparation ground, albeit at times a battleground, for the soul's learning." This from a wonderful book named Twin Souls, A Guide to finding your True Spiritual Partner. This is probably the best book on Twin Souls, ever written.

We have lived in so many earthly families. Around and around the karmic wheel we go, when it will stop, you never know. When will we stop reincarnating? Lady Magdalene explained that in this ascension process of exiting the 3rd dimension; that there will be no need to reincarnate any longer to have lessons. You are then graduated from the 3rd dimensional realm. Around the corner is your Heaven on Earth, that you have been waiting for, for centuries.

Let's honor ourselves. We have literally gone through hell, (*the valley of the shadow of death, … i.e. the moon's illusions*) and we have come out the other side! Recognize and own your accomplishments. Be joyful, for your success is great!

The Return of the Dove, a motion picture

Lady Magdalene finished her channeling sessions with us, with a wish. Her wish was that 'The Sharing Group' would see that her love for her twin soul, Jesus Christ/Sananda, (Esu Immanuel), would be expressed through music, and through a motion picture. We intend to honor her wish. A *'musical drama'* motion picture, is planned for release in 2008 or 2009. Our joy is overflowing as we embark on this challenging project. Her intention and hope is that her personal story of love, will inspire millions to heal and begin to share with her, the experiences that Heaven has to offer through Christ Consciousness.

It is Lady Magdalene's hope that certain music and certain actors are used in this film. We will follow her design very closely. In an enticing way, this film seeks to create an emotional activation within the hearts of its audience. We are excited and joyous to have this beautiful project introduced to us by Lady Magdalene. Her channeled messages are finished for now. The movie will be the next progression in picking up where these transmissions have left off. We look forward to this film's debut like enchanted children at Christmas time. Until we meet again, at the movie theater, bless you all!

We Love You!
The Sharing Group

Magdalene's Masada Perfume

for Healing & Heightened Sensitivity
to Divine Presence

Frankincense, Myrrh & Sandalwood, *the gift of The Magi*
Spikenard, *the gift of The Magdalene*
Rose Oil, *the gift of Mother Mary*

*Masada was the Essenes' Mountain Cave Fortress.

Anointing Your Holy Grail Body

"If the sun refused to shine,
I would still be loving you,
If mountains crumbled to the sea,
there would still be you and me."

-from a Led Zepphin song

To my Twin Soul

Through seasons of frozen pain,
to seasons of warm melting forgiveness,
our love has endured.
For eons of time we have braved changes well.
We are strong and tenacious now and forever,
and on this day I honor our bond.
It is eternal.
You are my reflection,
smiling back at me.
You are the kiss
that never ends.

-Sara Heartsong

☗ ☗ ✡ **17** ✡ ☗ ☗

Glossary of Terms &
References

Glossary of Terms

aeon
In Gnosticism a divine power or nature emanating from the Supreme Being and playing various roles in the operation of the universe.

archetype
An original model on which something is patterned, an example for people to follow

Ashtar Command
The unit of heavenly beings working under the command of the being named Ashtar, residing on the Starship Capricorn. Included in the Ashtar command: Sananda (Jesus), Archangel Michael and St Germain.

astrophysics or astrophysical
The branch of astronomy concerned with the physical nature of celestial bodies.

Atonement
Amends for a wrong or injury. Christian Theology, the reconciliation of God and mankind through the death of Jesus Christ.

Book of Mary
The Gospel of Mary Magdalene.

Christ Consciousness
Christ Consciousness is the level of ascension that humanity is currently evolving to. There are even higher levels, because evolution is endless. Through Jesus Christ humanity was blessed with an example of Christ Consciousness to follow. This example has been distorted through religion, however the restoration of Christ's original teachings is happened in these times.

Christ Consciousness Grid
A planetary grid is an etheric crystalline structure that envelops the planet and holds the consciousness of any one species of life. The Christ Consciousness Grid holds the vision or blueprint of Christ Consciousness for the planet.

Christ Group
The Christ Group consisted of Jesus, Mother Mary, all of his earth family members, Mary Magdalene, The Twelve Apostles, The Roman Centurion, the Celtic Druids, certain Zealots, certain Jewish people, the Essences, The Tat Brotherhood, Joseph of Arimathea, The Mystic Masters of the Far East, John the Baptist, the Angelic Realm and The Spiritual Hierarchy, and many more beings that are dedicated to the Planetary Ascension.

Christian Cults
Christian Cults tear down the member's current support networks and convince the members that their family, or their local community of Christian believers, is somehow ignorant, or corrupt, or not holy enough. They give the members a new support network and provide love and affirmation. They give "true revelations" available only to those in the group and encourage a feeling of pride in these new revelations. The manipulative motives usually provide ego gratification for the leader. Some cults can be dangerous.

Christ Michael
The Urantia Book states that Jesus came from another planet and there he is Christ Michael. Christ Michael shared the same physical body as Jesus. They are not the same being. Jesus came from Venus. Christ Michael is Aton, Creator Son of Nebadon

cosmogony
The branch of science concerned with the origin of the universe, especially the solar system.

Dodecahedron
The sacred geometry, three-dimensional shape having twelve plane faces.

dogma
An inflexible principle or set of principles laid down by an authority.

druid
A priest, magician, or soothsayer in the ancient Celtic religion.

Essene Brotherhood
300 immortal Egyptians joined the Tat Brotherhood and waited from roughly 1450 B.C. to about 500 B.C.-about 850 years or so, and then they migrated to a place called Masada Israel and they formed the Essene Brotherhood. Mother Mary was a part of the Essene Brotherhood and she was an immortal being.

Esu Immanuel
Another name of Jesus Sananda, or better known as Jesus Christ

First Contact
The landing of the 'Mother Ship' of Christ and the Celestials to begin the Golden Age

Gnostic Christianity
The branch of Christianity concerned with the unveiling of hidden truths, and based on the Gnostic Gospels and ancient Gnosticism.

Gnostic Gospels
The Gnostic Gospels is a way to explore the true teachings of Jesus and Mary Magdalene. There are five important Gnostic texts: The Gospel of Mary (Book of Mary), the Gospel of Truth, the Gospel of Thomas, the Gospel of Peter and the Gospel of Philip. They are all excluded from the Holy Bible.

Great White Brotherhood
A Spiritual Order of Hierarchy, an organization of Ascended Masters united for the highest purposes of God in man as set forth by Jesus the Christ, Gautama Buddha other World Teachers. The Great White Brotherhood also includes Members of the Heavenly Host, the Spiritual Hierarchy directly concerned with the evolution of our world, Beneficent Members from other planets that are interested in our welfare, as well as certain unascended chelas.

Hathors
A race of interdimensional, intergalactic beings from Venus. Get more details at **www.tomkenyon.com/hathors.php**

Holon of Balance
A tool of transformation used to stabilize energy and create balance during situations of confusion and discord. Get more details at **www.tomkenyon. com/hathors.php**

Holy Grail Vessel/The Body Temple
Embodying the Holy Grail. The concept of the Holy Grail within, with the understanding that your physical body is the Temple of the Soul.

Immortals
Once you have evolved through Ascension, you become immortal, meaning you won't age or ever have to go through the death process. The physical body becomes a Light Body that can change vibration at will and move through the universe at will. Ascended Masters can lower themselves to our vibration, so we can see them, however this rarely happens, because of the universal law of non-interference.

Knights Templar
A group of knights dating back to 1118 C.E. They started out as a monastic order but grew into a medieval institution all its own. Do you really think that the 'big secret' now, relates to just the Christ and Mary Magdalene Bloodline? Think again. Did you know that some of the Knights Templar members were traitors and were in cahoots with the Catholic Church's diabolical plans? Who will uncover the real secret? Perhaps the anti-christ motives of the secret

few, started their path to the new world order, for complete power and control, a very long time ago? Read this web-page: http://nesara.insights2.org/CrownTemplars.html think again.

lamentation
Deplorable or regrettable.

Lucifer Mind
The mind of illusion, an aspect of duality

macrocosm
The whole of a complex structure. The universe; the cosmos.

microcosm
Humankind regarded as the epitome of the universe. A thing regarded as encapsulating in miniature the characteristics of something much larger.

Masada
The mountain cave fortress of the Essene Brotherhood in the Holy Land

Mer-Ka-Ba Ascension Ship
'The Ancient Secret of The Flower of Life' (volume one) & (volume two) by Drunvalo Melchizedek, are great books that share metaphysical information related to Ascension and the Mer-Ka-Ba.

microcosmic

N.E.S.A.R.A.
A plan set up by the spiritual hierarchy, involving the intervention of Heaven to protect the innocence masses from the dark agendas of the anti-evolutionary forces. The need to expel these forces from this planet has become critical. Operation Nesara, the National Economic Security and Reformation Act, would provide billions of dollars to help humanity recover from the centuries of The Dark's heinous agendas. Through the Mother Earth's Ascension process major earthquakes may still happen. Nesara would be like the FEMA agency from Heaven providing funds to assist humanity in extreme emergency situations. Money for the poor, money for victims of natural disasters and money for humanitarian and environmental projects will relieve humanity from the heavy burdens created through duality. The time for unity is now.

Order of The Blue Rose
The people belonging to the group of Mother Mary's ministry. There are 72 sacred Orders that are associated with the Great White Brotherhood.

Order of The Magdalene
The people belonging to the group of Mary Magdalene's ministry. There are 72 sacred Orders that are associated with the Great White Brotherhood.

Orthodox Christianity

The belief that Christ's physical body literally rose to Heaven. In a Light Body*, this is possible, and He did rise. However Jesus did make the choice to remain on Earth so He lowered His vibration to do so, and live as a family man up into His senior years.

paranoia
A mental condition characterized by delusions of persecution, unwarranted jealousy, or exaggerated self-importance. Unjustified suspicion and mistrust of others.

pentagon
A plane figure with five straight sides and five angles.

Phoenix Journals
Jesus/Sananda speaks. At www.phoenixarchives.com you will find that the truth of our world history can be shocking.

Pistis Sophia
A Coptic book that was discovered in the late eighteenth century by Dr. A. Askew, an Englishman. The British Museum acquired the codex after his death. The importance of the *Pistis Sophia* is that it clearly establishes Mary Magdalene's role as an interlocutor, (a questioner). In Pistis Sophia, there is a total of 115 different questions and interpretations of Jesus' teachings by his followers. Of those, Mary Magdalene alone is responsible for asking 67 questions.

regent
The one who rules during the absence of the sovereign.

Rabboni
A Jewish teacher/master. Mary Magdalene often called Jesus her Rabonni. A term of endearment and honor.

Sacrament of The Last Supper by Salvador Dali: view painting at www.ellens-place.net/dali.html

sacrifice of the Age of Pisces
The theme of the Age of Pisces, imposed upon us in that time frame.

Saint Germain
The Ascended Master Saint Germain, known for the Violet Flame of transformation and The 'I Am ' activity. He was once called the '*Wonder Man of Europe*' and he was instrumental in the creation of the Constitution of the United States of America.

Sananda
Another name of Jesus

Seven Veils

The dance of the seven veils, the dance of duality, was intended to teach us about removing these (evils), these illusions that are the energy veils that keep us in duality consciousness.

The 'seven veils' lesson taught by Christ was greatly misunderstood and was carried into the future as the myth of Jesus casting out seven devils from Mary Magdalene. In truth she was the only one who understood the concept of the 'seven energy veils' lesson.

777 Portal of The Mystical Marriage

Twin Flame Reunion with dedication to serving God and Humanity. See www.thequantumawakening.com

Shadow Termination

This term created by Kryon, and it relates to the Book of Revelations. Read page 276 to page 287 in Kryon Book V11.

Sophia

Mythic aspect of Mary Magdalene relating to The Magdalene's entrapment in the lower dimensions of duality, with the eventual release and return to Heaven, however that Heaven is to be on Earth! Her release is linked with Humanity release of duality and reawakening to full consciousness.

sovereign

The one possessing the supreme power and authority in a state, in this case the entire planet.

Spiritual Hierarchy

The Spiritual Hierarchy is composed of beings that have been given the responsibility for organizing and running the governmental positions of the universes. Ascended masters, The Angels, representatives from other galaxies and Jesus and Mary Magdalene is included in this Spiritual Hierarchy.

sublime

Inspiring awe, an ultimate example of something.

Tat Brotherhood

Another name for the Great White Brotherhood.

The Magdalene

All facets of Mary Magdalene. All aspects of her multi-dimensional soul working for the Light.

Trinitarianism

Christian doctrine stressing belief in the Trinity.

Triple Mary Goddesses

Mother Mary, *embodiment of The Divine Mother*, Quan Yin, *daughter of the East*, and Mary Magdalene, *daughter of the West*, are united in purpose and service to humanity. They are Spiritual Female Leaders for today. Ask the Trinity

Mary Masters of Compassion to help you, and to bring endless compassion and loving kindness to all souls everywhere.

Both Mary Magdalene and Quan Yin had fathers who believed their daughters were evil, and this misunderstanding relates to the gross error of the ways of patriarchy.

twin soul/twin flame:

The twin soul or twin flame is your equal, yet opposite double, the other half of your soul, however two halves will not make a twin soul merging. In other words what is required for this most exquisitely beautiful union to occur is the spiritual development that comes through eons of time. The masculine and feminine aspects within both individuals must be developed. The melding then becomes two wholes merging into one again. Many are ripe and ready for this reunion in these times.

Vesica Piscis

The symbol of *twin soul merging* is the vesica piscis. The two developed whole individuals (symbolized as two circles) merge back into one.

Violet Flame

A tool of transformation. Free yourself of discord and imperfection by visualizing the purifying Violet Flame of Saint Germain. Feel the Flame passing through the body and around it.

War in The Mind

see Lucifer Mind

White Dragon

A mythic term for a Protector of Doves. A Dove is an archetype of innocence, peace and purity.

Zealot

A member of an ancient Jewish sect aiming at a world Jewish theocracy and resisting the Romans until ad 70.

References:

Page 4 The Hathor Material: Messages from an Ascended Civilization, by Tom Kenyon & Virginia Essene

Page 125, 125 *Twin Souls, A Guide to Finding Your True Spiritual Partner*, by Patricia Joudry & Maurie Pressman

Page 118 *I Remember Union*, by Flo Calhaun

The Only Planet of Choice, by Phyllis V. Schlemmer

The healing workbook by Sharon Riegie Maynard, of Washington, USA

Recommended Websites

What's Up on Planet Earth: www.whatsuponplanetearth.com
Karen Bishop has published great books on The Ascension process

Gail Swanson is a wise and loving Mary Magdalene educator. Her website is
www.theheartoflove.com

An exercise for healing your inner child with Master Jesus: www.indecontent.
com/lightweaver click on channellings, left-hand side of page, then 5D Heart
Chakra Activation

www.radicalforgiveness.com

Jessica Wilson is a clairvoyant healer and teacher at www.creativefire.org

Sharon Riegie Maynard is a healer, writer and a powerful woman working for
positive political change. www.sisterspace.net

I.E.T., *Integrated Energy Therapy Practitioner,* Lauren Gorgo:
Heal with The Angels & Your Spirit Guides www.thinkwithyourheart.net

Free Online Cosmic Newsletters: www.thequantumawakening.com

Eleven Steps of Ascension www.star-esseenia.org

The Christ Matrix www.christmatrix.com

Sound Healing www.universalsong.net

The Visionary Art of Marius Michael-George, at www.mariusfineart.com

The University of Metaphysical Sciences
www.umsonline.org

The Visionary Art of Suzanne De Veuve
www.suzannedeveuve.com

The Light Movie
www.lightmovie.com

Recommended Books for Healing and Ascension

Twin Souls *A Guide to Finding Your True Spiritual Partner,*
by Patricia Joudry & Maurie Pressman

All of the Kyron Books by Lee Carroll

The Ancient Secret of the Flower of Life volume 1 &11
Drunvalo Melchizedek

Sananda on Telepathy

Recommended Movies for
Healing, Information and Ascension

The Da Vinci Code
The Secret
Contact
What The Bleep Do We Know?
Seven People You Meet in Heaven

Movies about twin flames:

Always, Holly Hunter & Richard Drefuss
What Dreams May Come, Robin Williams

and in the future …
The movie based from this book!
Stay tuned at www.angelmatrix.net for details.

🕯️🕯️ ✡ **18** ✡ 🕯️🕯️

In Conclusion

Sharing?

In conclusion, we remember John F Kennedy, saying, "Ask not what your country can do for you, ask what you can do for your country." What can we do for our countries, for our humanity, for our Father in Heaven, and for our Mother the Earth?

Lady Magdalene:

Yes, thank you, get involved! Just your awareness has the power to move mountains. I am blessed to have you as part of this awesome team of God's shining servants for goodness and peace. The fact is that Jesus Saves, but only if you are willing to do most of the work. *A lazy humanity* is not acceptable.

What I would like to see on this planet are more nonprofit organizations that are highly effective. Now without sounding accusatory remember that the spell of prestige and power is still a strong issue on this planet. Beware of overpriced worship clubs that feed ego gratification instead of performing simple good deeds to help others. It might help to examine the resume of an organization before you blindly trust that their motives are pure.

Perhaps the energy of Truth will inspire many good deeds of man. Perhaps your scientists will finally stop spending tons of money on trying to prove that the Ascension was real. How many meals at the Salvation Army could be made from the money that has been spent on examining the *Shroud of Turin*? That is a lot of loaves and fishes folks. What more proof do you want? The proof is in your Holy Grail Heart. Perhaps more physical proof will unearth? So be it, if it is the will of God!

Know this about technology, the danger lies in the hearts of men who abuse technology to hurt people. Remember that the twin to power is responsibility. Perhaps humanity will never set off another bomb. Erase your *Armageddon Nightmares*. Perhaps no one ever told you that *Armageddon* does not have to happen! Propaganda says ongoing war is inevitable. My heart says you have been tricked into believing that. The ways of God, through technology, can save your planet. The ways of men at war can destroy it.

Be the brother or sister that Christ would count on to uphold honor, dignity, empowerment, healthy living and peace for all. Many new healing tools and higher technologies are unveiling and research and development in these arenas is badly needed. Lack of money for these things should not exist, but in ignorance, there has been extreme abuse of power and money, causing a social disheartening and discouragement, beyond believe. Shine your Light upon the dark waters of deceit and the injustices that create perpetual suffering of the sick and the poor.

Please value the spiritual, cultural and religious customs of all peoples of the world. No form of worship should be exterminated, out of pure judgment that their way is not correct. The seeding, of the races of humanity, comes from the whole universe. Do not think that any race or people, do not have the right to be here!

Know that America, a melting pot of diverse cultures, has an important part to play through *democracy*. The purposes of freedom and empowerment were birthed in the writing of the constitution of the United States of America. Saint Germain* of the Great White Brotherhood* and all the writers of the constitution were fulfilling the will of God.

Democracy is highly revered by God, and even the decisions about this planet are made in a democratic fashion. We highly suggest that Americans protect their freedom and democracy by becoming politically active. Look for the work of brave new films and books in the years to come. Your world is buzzing with change.

The ones who have stored away riches might want to ask themselves, what a better world might do for their *safety deposit box, called the Earth,* which is the world that everyone has to live in. The environmental errors you have made can be corrected. The solutions through love and generosity can save this planet and make it a shining success in the eyes of many advanced civilizations that have their attention on you. We are the freewheeling adventurous types, and in this 'movie' we are playing all the parts. Everyone in the universe is watching so get outrageous in your love and courage and participate! I love you.

Your Ascended Lady Mary Magdalene,
Your Sister Aimee,
Your Goddess Isis,
Your Lady Nada
Your Female Christ,
The Eternal Twin Flame of Jesus Christ.

Dear Courageous Souls
May no good heart be denied,
let the miracles flow with a group mind intention,
to include everyone in your
World Peace & Well-Being Prayers,
and for a middle eastern woman deeply laden
with grief and shame,
may the shackles be removed,
and may we give back to her, what was stolen from her.
For the starving children,
may we feed every one of them,
so their bodies may develop correctly,
so they may grow into healthy men and women.
May the Princesses & Princes of Light & Bliss,
receive their missing link to Full Bliss & Godspeed,
their Twin Flame, Soul Counterpart,
and may no one be denied!
No one with an open heart shall be denied.

-Lady Magdalene

Evolution For Eventual Utopia

A Message from The Sharing Group

At the close of our channeled messages with Mary Magdalene, we were so touched by her love and compassion for humanity. With her eloquent grace, a sense of humor and a nonjudgmental approach we learned so much from her. We honor her and with *Good Courage* we intend to act on the concepts expressed by her. Gratitude and joy is expressed from 'The Sharing Group' for being a part of this learning experience. We hope that what you have learned through this transmission from Mary Magdalene, will bring you closer to your own *Christ Heart* and to God.

May a deeper love and understanding now live in your thoughts regarding this amazing woman Mary Magdalene, the real wife of Jesus Christ. She shares an eternal relationship with the Beloved Jesus. May the *Peace of the Dove* enter your heart to overfill your *Holy Grail with Crystal Clear Consciousness*. Like a child full of glowing wonder, be of good faith and peace. We bless you in your *Eternal Life*, which is The Creator's gift for every soul!

In closing we would like to thank the beautiful woman Sara Heartsong, the channeler of Lady Magdalene. She channeled Mary Magdalene with crystal clarity. Her anonymity, we will protect at her request. She would like to say that in was an honor to channel Lady Magdalene for the world and she hopes that the information will be well received.

The Sharing Group's Favorite Humanitarians

Lady Diana,
Her work with helping AIDS sufferers was truly heroic, and her saintly actions, plus her beauty and grace will never be forgotten.

Nelson Mandala,
Remember his famous speech to South Africa. It is at http://mom-camp.com/recommend/spirituality.htm

Moshe Dayan
If you want to make peace, you don't talk to your friends. You talk to your enemies.

John F Kennedy
I see little of more importance to the future of our country and of civilization than full recognition of the place of the artist.
If art is to nourish the roots of our culture, society must set the artist free to follow his vision wherever it takes him.

Henry David Thoreau
A man is rich in proportion to the things he can afford to let alone.

Jon Lennon
There will be an answer.....Let it be.

Marilyn Monroe
Hollywood's a place where they'll pay you a thousand dollars for a kiss, and fifty cents for your soul.

Kahlil Gibran
God has given you a spirit with wings on which to soar into the spacious firmament of Love and Freedom. Is it not pitiful then that you cut your wings with your own hands and suffer your soul to crawl like an insect upon the earth?

Helen Keller
Tolerance … is the greatest gift of the mind; it requires the same effort of the brain that it takes to balance oneself on a bicycle.

Albert Einstein
Imagination is more important than knowledge.

William Shakespeare
The lunatic, the lover and the poet, Are of imagination all compact.

Leonardo Da Vinci
Nature never breaks her own laws.

The Buddha
It is wrong to think that misfortunes come from the east or from the west; they originate within one's own mind. Therefore, it is foolish to guard against misfortunes from the external world and leave the inner mind uncontrolled

Rwandan Proverb
You can out-distance that which is running after you, but not what is running inside you.

The Buddha
When a man has pity on all living creatures, then only is he noble.

Dalai Lama
Remember that *not* getting what you want is sometimes a wonderful stroke of luck.

Jesus Christ
Except ye become as little children, ye shall not enter the kingdom of heaven.

Jesus Christ
His Most Important Commandments,
'Hear, O Israel, the Lord our God, the Lord is one. Love the Lord your God with all your heart and with all your soul and with all your mind and with all your strength. The second is this: Love your neighbor as yourself. There is no commandments greater that these.'

Mother Teresa
I know God will not give me anything I can't handle. I just wish that He didn't trust me so much.

Mary Poppins
A spoonful of sugar helps the medicine go down.

Anne Frank
In spite of everything, I still believe that people are really good at heart.

Martin Luther King, Jr.
We must learn that passively to accept an unjust system is to cooperate with that system, and thereby to become a participant in its evil.

The Parable of The Spoons

A holy man was having a conversation with the Lord one day and said, "Lord, I would like to know what Heaven and Hell are like. "The Lord led the holy man to two doors. He opened one of the doors and the holy man looked in. In the middle of the room was a large round table. In the middle of the table was a large pot of stew, which smelled delicious and made the holy man's mouth water. The people sitting around the table were thin and sickly. They appeared to be famished. They were holding spoons with very long handles and each found it possible to reach into the pot of stew and take a spoonful, but because the handle was longer than their arms, they could not get the spoons back into their mouths. The holy man shuddered at the sight of their misery and suffering. The Lord said, "You have seen Hell." They went to the next room and opened the door. It was exactly the same as the first one. There was the large round table with the large pot of stew which made the holy man's mouth water. The people were equipped with the same long-handled spoons, but here the people were well nourished and plump, laughing and talking. The holy man said, "I don't understand." "It is simple" said the Lord, "it requires but one skill. You see, they have learned to feed each other. While the greedy think only of themselves, a friend is someone who reaches for your hand, and touches your heart."

Mary Magdalene's Ascension Prayer

Forgive, Release, Transmute,
all past traumas and dramas.
Know you are worthy to receive
God's Great Gifts.
Become the child,
Laughing with wild abandonment,
and playing in ecstasy.

The Veils between Worlds are lifting
and our loved ones are landing
within the hearts of those
ready to leap forth.
This quickening,
this opening to wonder, is here,
so have no fear when we come near,
just embrace Us and know
that Mother Earth and Father Sky,
are joining to embrace you,
The Christ Children,
and The Reunited Twin Flames
are standing like strong pillars.

God's Great Sea of Love
is ready to break the
Illusionary Dam of Damnation,
thus insuring our Salvation,
and entrance into Eternal life.

The Brides and the Bridegrooms,
Are joining in rapturous reunion.
And the waves of Father's Love,
are washing over us
so long no more,
Now Love may pour,
And heal and cleanse,
And feed and nourish.

May Utopia start.
and beating as one
heart,
Let us Celebrate
The Promise of God, Fulfilled,
Resurrection into Eternal Life,
on an Ascended Planet Earth,
May Christ Return
with Christ Consciousness,
Alive in Everyone's Heart

Emotional Body Healing & Reconnecting with God

This book excerpt is from Sharon Maynard's emotional body healing workbook. It has been added to this chapter to help teach you about the core issues of co-dependency, with its dysfunctional human behaviors. The modern day evils of years of oppressive and stunned human development have taken its toll on humanity. The goal here is to give the masses an easy understanding of why our world is emotionally dis-eased and how we can quickly and easily heal these issues.

What is at the core of dis-ease:

Where Our Core Dis-Ease Has Lead

A) The introduction of fear onto planet Earth has distorted Universal energy. Distorted or negative energy has accumulated over lifetimes. It surrounds the planet and acts to blind our Spiritual senses. Because of this density, all souls birthing onto this planet have an inherent sense of separation from Source.

B) The circulatory systems of our physical body, have been rewired to prevent access to our identity and purpose. This has caused an additional emptiness within. In our aloneness, we reach out to find ways to fill the hole.

C) Because reaching out can never fill the hole (make us whole), these external relationships escalate the sense of loneliness and rejection. Reality becomes harsh. Individuals create other ways to survive; memory loss, frozen emotions, burnout, survival mentality, expressing the inner pain through violence, abuse, etc.

D) Behaviors that cover this greater pain are physical illness, mental illness, compulsions, addictions, putting on 'perfect' coverings in which to hide, i.e. hair, clothing, houses, children, religions, etc.

E) At some point, the suppressed pain slips through. We then have situations that are unmanageable; our job ends, our relationships fall apart, our children misbehave, our physical body is 'dis-eased' and life becomes chaotic.

Dysfunctional Behavior

When an individual feels disconnected from Source (God) there is a deep sorrow and anger. The reversals in energy circuitry prevent a connection to one's Divine Identity. With no identity, we feel deeply injured and lacking. One goes through life with no needs or wants, constantly sacrificing or at the other end of the scale, demanding that everyone know what we need or want and give it to us. One feels an inner drying up from too much time spent away from the soul's *spirit*. This inner core of emptiness manifests on the planet in pretty predictable ways.

As children and then adults, we try to avoid this harsh reality because it is interspersed with pain. Life becomes full of stress and the harder you work, the more chaotic life becomes. There are many ways of dulling the pain. Some we know as addictions, others as physical illness, mental illness, etc.

List of Dysfunctional Behaviors:

people pleasing, perfectionism, resentment, over commitment, striving for power, physical or mental illness, loss of personal morality, tolerating sexual abuse, indecisiveness, blaming others for your reality, taking responsibility for the reality of others, lack of passion, pushing others to be your higher power, expecting others to see you as their higher power, expressing feelings explosively, lying, controlling the reality of others, shutting others out, helplessness, irresponsibility, inappropriate social behavior, extreme problem solving, score-keeping, lack of intimacy, financial problems, inadequate or un-fulfilling sex life, jealousy, name-calling, arguing about facts, always having to be right (or wrong), self-centeredness or insisting people have your value system.

It is important to observe the ways you alter your moods or try to feel better. As you reach for outer forms such as food, work, drugs, sex, relationships, or spiritual pursuits, is it to dull pain or fill the emptiness? To what degree are you able to go within, and fill the *holes* with *Spiritual Wholeness* and then create forms and activities to celebrate and express your inner sense of personal beauty?

Now For A Symbol

Now I challenge you to run with these scissors
and cut the energy connections to all past feelings of sadness, despair, hopelessness,
apathy, self-hatred and_____ _____add your own to the list.

With those cords cut, you should feel a lot better.
Now go run on the beach with your dog; it's a sunny
day and the birds and the streams, care not for sadness.

The fairies play, Pan makes music and all is well.
All is well. Choose your symbols well.
The Enigma of your card sweep can guide you,
A Gypsy Queen, Dancing Free?
Who do you, want to be?

Thanks to Sara Heartsong, the world now has a much greater understanding of who Mary Magdalene was and how important her relationship to Jesus/ Sananda is, because they are both spiritual teachers, healers, and twin souls. As they prepare to return physically, to the planet, we should be preparing to receive them anew. How will we accomplish that? First, we must realize how church dogma has shrouded their true teachings. These masks of falseness will hopefully fall away gracefully.

As this book was getting ready to go to press, we got a call from Sara Heartsong. She was concerned that she would miss telling us of the one last channeled message from Lady Magdalene, which she failed to hear before. What did she fail to hear and why? I will explain. The angels gladly helped her remove *a program* that causes women to block out trauma, yet hold in trauma, and remain trapped in its sadness, without knowing why. Sara's trauma related to Magdalene's trauma. Sara had blocked a past life memory of a traumatic miscarriage she experienced.

Sara's memory surfaced, and the energy of the pain and the trauma of the experience, was released to The Mother Earth for healing, with the help of The Angels. Then Lady Magdalene's last message surfaced.

Lady Magdalene says to Sara:
I have been wanting to tell you about the story of why 'The Father' allowed Christ to return to me after the Resurrection and have a married life with me. With deep mercy and grace the special and unusual dispensation was granted to heal my trauma. The trauma I speak of was a miscarriage I had in a sea cave on the coast of Southern France.

I will tell you now that I was so distraught over the thought of The Mission being 'miscarried' into the future. My symbolic 'miscarriage', related to my feelings that Christ's Movement, would be 'miscarrying'(misunderstood) into the future. My pain related to my personal torment over the imperfection of certain apostles with their limited understanding. However, within imperfection lies perfection awaiting to be born at a later time. That time is now.

Our first child was conceived when Christ and I were at The Waterfall. We went to the waterfall and slipped out of time. As I mentioned before we left on this trip, to heal from my stoning and to accept the heavy weight of our coming fate; The Act of Atonement*, The Crucifixion/Resurrection, that would soon be upon us to accomplish.

Our heart flames merged and became one as the falling water caressed us and then with a sudden breath we flew out of our bodies, up into The Heavens. This merging, this Ascension, so Divine; how could we not conceive a child, it was as natural as breathing. By whose rule, did we stray from our duty to The Father?

What did this universe expect of me? If I were not supposed to be human, then why would God send me to this reality? Perhaps uplifting this world meant becoming a master of patience and acceptance? I was so human just like anybody else and in a bewildering paradox I was a Goddess of Love for my Godman, my Lionheart of amazing courage and curiosity. I was just the girl next door trapped in the illusions of the times and in the case of the Holy Land back then; morbid, cruel, competitive, warlike and patriarchal Roman rule.

A miscarriage often occurs in nature, when the fetus cannot develop properly, due to the ill health of the mother. The shock and trauma to my body's systems, weeks before and after the Crucifixion/Resurrection led nature to take her course. The turbulent sea, carried our boat, led by The Angels to the shore. Why was I on that boat? I was hiding from my trauma, attempting to run from an illusionary fate, that was a lie. Whose lie? What lie? The lie that others led me to believe about myself. I will leave it at that.

In the Gulf of The Lion, the lamb lied down, emotionally broken beyond consoling.

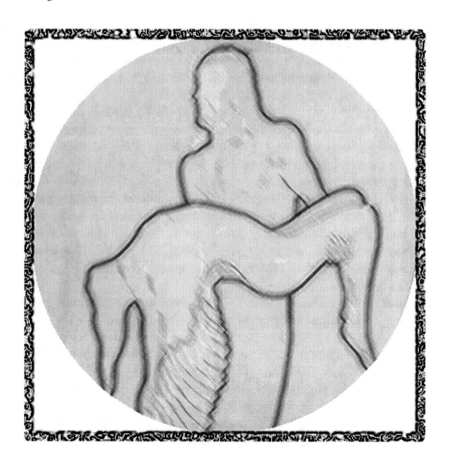

Christ's Ascension was truly a blessed miracle, however the reactions of the apostles to this miracle, I never would have though, would have caused so much distension and distrust. Negativity set in, with The Apostles arguing and not really absorbing the Miracle that took place.

I felt like my anchor, My Rabboni, my whole reason to push on, in the name of Love, in a society of violence, jealousy and hatred, was being torn from me in a cruel way. The darkest days of my life, were those weeks that followed Christ's Ascension and in my emotional state of severe trauma the child in my womb did not survive.

How could she still be born? She came back and she was born through my pregnancy that followed, after Jesus and I moved to Kashmir. Her true name is Mercy. God's gift to me, my husband Jesus, was a testament of God's Deep Mercy and Compassion.

God's Loving Christ Council Beings concurred that my sacrifices became out of balance when the darkness sunk into my soul on the days that followed my miscarriage. Joseph of Arimathea carried me out of the cave of darkness, where the blood of the lamb spilled. He carried me straight into the Light of God's Love, into the arms of my Beloved. We exiled to Kashmir, secretly.

Jesus was waiting for me in my bed chamber. His long journey to Kashmir was over and our new life began with utmost joy in our hearts. I remember being reborn in that first moment when I saw him and he tenderly embraced me, as my tears of joy and mercy flowed. "Will you Marry me, my Mary?", spoke the man with the child in his eyes, the human man Jesus, who so graciously and flawlessly upheld His duty to God and exemplified how every human can become a divine human; but not through some special advantage or Elite status. Only through the heart, only through the heart; that is where the jewel is. And He said I was 'The Rock' that kept him anchored to The Mission. Funny, but he was mine too.

Christ loved me so much that The Father would not deny us our union, our normal life, that we so deserved after all that we went through. The apostles may have fallen short of their highest potential, causing a part of a potential plan (My leadership over the apostles, as 2nd Christ, with Jesus Christ in the ascended state). So what. Everyone has fallen short of highest potential. It happens every day. But the opportunity to change direction exists in every moment. So please don't think that I hold old grudges against the apostles! I loved them dearly, and I always will. Their destinies; to exemplify certain archetypes was fulfilled. What can we learn now about Faith and Equality through their example? Remember the testament *through The Book of Mary? Levi defended my honor and place in Christ's life; and bless him for doing so.*

Jesus Christ loved me in that life in every way imaginable! That is why I will treasure the life I lived as Mary Magdalene forever! Every moment was perfect; ever the traumas served as teachers, that initiated me into the acceptance of My Greatness and Oneness with God. I will forever serve you as your sister, as your friend and as your teacher if need be. WE are all great! WE ARE ALL ONE! WE ARE ALL GOD!
Jesus Christ taught me how to join him as his equal. Will you join me as your Equal? Will you accept this magic miracle, my dear Holy Grail Sisters and Brothers?

So, yes I did travel in a boat with Joseph of Arimathea, after the Crucifixion/ Resurrection. In my trauma over my turbulent relationship with Christ's apostles, I decided to hide in the boat that landed miraculously on the shore in France. The Christ bloodline of France? Well, let me just say this, The *Holy Genetics of Christ Bloodline* is in everyone, because we are all of the soul lineage of God. Following the Lineage from the outside, won't help birth everyone into Christ Consciousness! Will you help Christ and I bring all the Christ Children Home? Will you accept this gracious invitation?

Jesus & Magdalene in Kashmir

Jesus:
I can see the future my Mary. It's the End Times and
in a treasure hunting frenzy they look for you
and I.....everywhere but within?
Magdalene:
Maybe if I tell them my life story,
stripped of all the veils of many perspectives,
maybe then they will understand,
and then they will shift
and take flight like butterflies?
Jesus:
.....ok then my darling.... and so it will be....
.....*lets go back to sleep.*

Magdalene's Gift & Lesson

To Teach that Love is Innocence and to Learn that Love is Trust, Grounded in Discernment

Jesus spoke in parables and he also had a 'parable type' nickname for many of his followers. He used to call me his 'little pigeon'. This term of endearment will always be precious to my heart. Like a child, I was totally open and willing to learn from him. However, I was at a stage in my development that lacked discernment; in other words, I was naive. If you look up pigeon in the dictionary, you will find that its slang meaning is, 'one who is easy duped'. The men, who envied my close relationship with the Savior, found that it was easy to discourage me and trick me with thoughts that Jesus did not really love me, and he could never make a commitment to me, because he was 'married to God'. They followed the patriarchal programming of that time and then added their own desire to deify The Savior.

The feud between myself and certain apostles, caused a deep wounding in my heart, that led me to have a miscarriage. However, in my fragile state, I was shown the magnificence of God's Mercy & Grace, when Jesus asked me to marry him. I vowed to someday teach others how much mercy and grace God bestows on the faithful.

Know that I was never a victim. The illusions of betrayal were part of my incarnations into duality lives. In those lives much suffering and victimization taught me well that duality is not God's will. Now is the time for God's will and gifts, and these gifts are for you to dear sisters and brothers. Know that all is forgiven and I love you Peter.

I am so relieved to be 'all grown up now'. I am still quite childlike and sometimes naive, while in a body, but this is due to my high hopes that everyone is good at heart. Although most people are totally good at heart, some people have quite a track record for manipulating others to get what they want. This can be hurtful to those who would never dream of being that way, and therefore misread people. And so the road to clear discernment is long. I needed a lot of lives to master discernment.

Humility is the cornerstone of the Christ Vibration. Accepting your divine greatness, must live in the humble view of one's own importance. This paradox allows one to know that we are all equal in the eyes of God. We are all born with the same potential to actualize our divine blueprint. How far we develop this is our own choice. Jesus was guided by many experiences that honed his humility. To carry the Humble Christ Vibration into the future he had to learn it and live it. So as far as understanding the importance of the human Jesus who married, had several children and lived to be over one hundred, well there you have it, a well developed resume to hold The Christ Vibration into the future. The future 'Christed Humanity' will learn that it is not about worshiping Jesus Christ, it is about being a Christ who also holds no desire to be above any other. This 'circle way'; this 'spiral dance' continues on into eternity. Enjoy! You have only just begun, to truly live.

This is a glorious time for us all and I am looking forward to meeting you in the future. I bless you on your journey into full Christ Consciousness. God Loves You!
Godspeed
   Lady Magdalene
    The White Dove

PS-It was pure joy to share with you!

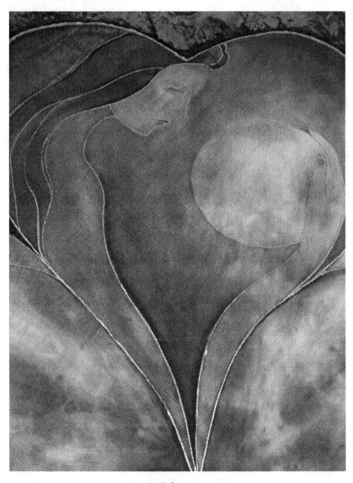

Gaia's Heart

HUMAN ANGELS HELPING HUMANKIND, a free monthly newsletter at: www.angelmatrix.net

Lady Magdalene Workshop Kits Available through www.angelmatrix.info

The Magdalene Workshop Kits

Have Fun, Heal and Learn about Mary Magdalene!
Have your own healing workshop with this lovely kit containing:

- A copy of 'An Honest Talk with Mary Magdalene: Freedom Through Christ Consciousness'
- White Silk Altar Cloth with bells
- The Diamond Gateway CD, a guided Mary Magdalene meditation by Gail Swanson
- A booklet of instructions for the workshop
- Lady Magdalene's Masada Essential Oils: Sample sizes of five different pure essential oils: Rose Otto, Frankincense, Myrrh, India Sandalwood and Spikenard

The essential oils are for inducing the energy of The Sacred Marriage of the Divine Male and the Divine Female within, thus opening the gateway to Twin Soul Reunion. Heal the heart with forgiveness and compassion. Open to Divine Love. Soothe anxiety, stress and trauma associated with The Planetary Ascension.

Heal the Christ Child Within and create the New Earth.

Discover the mysteries of The Magdalene through this affordable workshop kit. You will educate yourself and your invited guesses. The Ascended Lady Mary Magdalene has powerful tools to help transform your world on an individual level and on a planetary level. The Magdalene would like to stress that The Ascended Masters are Humanitarians, here in these times to assist you in rebuilding your world. As all life rises, rejoice and give gratitude. Using this workshop kit, learn, heal and have fun in a powerful way.

Explore the Mysteries of The Magdalene with your friends in your hometown.

Sheranda Tay
Angel Matrix International

Closing thoughts from Sara & Sheranda

Draining another's energy as demonstrated in the movie 'The Celestine Prophecy' has perpetuated the dysfunctional theme of planet Earth. In the healed New Earth humans will freely give the love energy that they discover within. Through drawing love energy from Source (God) humans will no longer need to steal energy from each other. Controlling other people and sucking off their energy or allowing another to suck off your energy or control you, are dysfunctional behaviours. When humans learn to connect back to the God source and they give love energy freely, the next step for them will be to transform into their Light Bodies. The movie called 'The Celestine Prophecy' demonstrates this very well. The Bible in 'Revelations' describes people disappearing. Perhaps the correct understanding of this is that the Light Body is invisible in the 3rd dimension, and once you are in the higher dimension, through *birthing your own Christ Light within*, then you will have done what Jesus did. This is perhaps what Jesus meant by saying; you will someday do what I have done and more. As Magdalene educators we truly believe that Jesus was trying to empower you in saying this.

It is also important to understand that 'Christ Consciousness', or *birthing the Christ Light within*, refers to a level of consciousness and there are even higher levels of consciousness. The *crystal stairway of consciousness* is endless. Now it does not matter if you are a Christian or a Buddhist, or _____(add whatever you like in the blank space) because this is not about following a certain religion, it is about accepting Divine Love and an experiential connection to God. It is about realizing that you are creating your own reality. Jesus' highest vision was to help humanity experience a shift in perception, which included an appreciation for our oneness with God.

Sara and I never had a negative experience with the Christian religion, however we know people who did and some of them have quite an aversion to Jesus based on their family's suppressive religious beliefs during childhood. Sara and I would like to say that suppressive, controlling or patriarchal are not the ways of the real Jesus. Perhaps you could help us teach the truth about the radical God-man who loved women as equals and advocated peace and freedom. Perhaps you could also help us teach the truth about the radical Magdalene who would like to see men heal from '*The Battle of the Sexes*', as well as women.

It was not God's plan to have men build religions that would become corrupt. The *duality experience* was not meant to last forever. The time to graduate from the duality experience is now! It is your free-will choice to embrace this graduation into eternal life and freedom. Freewill is a gift from God and only you can make the choice to release yourself from Lucifer's prison. What have we learned through the domination of the masses through suppressive forms of religion? What are we learning about manipulation and lies through the now fake democracy of America?

The ways of Christ Consciousness bring eternal life and freedom. Chose wisely, my dear brothers and sisters, and know that the heart of The Magdalene united with Jesus, support you in opening up to Divine Love and Light which is Truth. May all beings be happy, empowered and free.

Sara Heartsong & Sheranda Tay

ABOUT THE AUTHOR

The Messenger, Sara Heartsong is the mother, healer and messenger who channeled Mary Magdalene for this book. She holds the credentials of an old soul, grounded in wisdom and love. Her prerequisites are life experience which developed her deep compassion for humanity. With the help of co-author Sheranda Tay this blessed book came into reality.

Co-author Sheranda Tay is a Visionary Silk Artist and Mary Magdalene educator. She has researched the subject of Mary Magdalene and the Holy Grail for twenty-two years. She wrote a metaphysical college elective course on the subject of Mary Magdalene for The University of Metaphysical Sciences. Sara chose Sheranda to bring these channeled messages of Mary Magdalene to the world through this book.

To preserve the integrity of the channeled words of Mary Magdalene they were not altered through an editorial process. Mary Magdalene asked that we not be concerned about the literary merits of this book. The importance of simplicity was accentuated by Mary Magdalene because the Holy Grail Legends have become so complex. Mary Magdalene's messages are for truth seeking people of all age groups. The coming Planetary Ascension and how it relates to The Holy Grail is for all to understand.

978-0-595-45882-0
0-595-45882-3

Printed in the United States
94011LV00002B/1/A

9 780595 458820